Grade 1

I CAN MAKE IT!
I CAN READ IT!

20 Reproducible Booklets to Develop Early Literacy Skills

FALL

WRITTEN BY:
Nancy Anderson, Linda Morgason, Jan Robbins

EDITED BY:
Mary Lester
Kim T. Griswell

ILLUSTRATED BY:
Mary Lester

COVER DESIGN BY:
Nick Greenwood and Kimberly Richard

CHILDREN'S AND PARENTS' SERVICES
PATCHOGUE-MEDFORD LIBRARY

www.themailbox.com

©2000 by THE EDUCATION CENTER, INC.
All rights reserved.

ISBN# 1-56234-391-2

Except as provided for herein, no part of this publication may be reproduced or transmitted in any form or by any means, electronic or mechanical, including photocopying, recording, or storing in any information storage and retrieval system or electronic online bulletin board, without prior written permission from The Education Center, Inc. Permission is given to the original purchaser to reproduce patterns and reproducibles for individual classroom use only and not for resale or distribution. Reproduction for an entire school or school system is prohibited. Please direct written inquiries to The Education Center, Inc., P.O. Box 9753, Greensboro, NC 27429-0753. The Education Center®, *The Mailbox*®, and the mailbox/post/grass logo are registered trademarks of The Education Center, Inc. All other brand or product names are trademarks or registered trademarks of their respective companies.

Manufactured in the United States
10 9 8 7 6 5 4 3 2

TABLE OF CONTENTS

Let's Get Ready for School! 3

Binky Rides the Bus! (Bus Safety) 7

A Friend to Grow With 13

All About Me! 15

Who Helps Me? 21

Around My Neighborhood 25

The Four Seasons 28

All Dolled Up! (Months of the Year) 36

In the Tree 42

A Tasty Poem 46

Dalmatian Dolly's Safety Rules (Fire Safety) 50

Mr. Owl 54

Let's Go Batty! 59

The Busy Spider 64

Hello, Mr. Scarecrow! 70

One Dark Night 75

Native American Rock Art 80

Pilgrim Children 86

Gobble! Gobble! What's for Lunch? 88

Time for Harvest! 92

LET'S GET READY FOR SCHOOL!

What better way to start the school year off than with this fun-packed interactive booklet! Give each student a copy of pages 4–6. Read the booklet pages with students. Then instruct each student to color the bookbag, pocket, and school supplies. Next, direct the student to stack his pages in numerical order and staple them to the bookbag. To attach the pocket, have the student spread glue on the bookbag where indicated and press the pocket onto the glued area. When the glue has dried, provide time for each student to read his completed booklet to a partner. As the student reads about a school supply, he places the matching object in his bookbag pocket. After sufficient practice reading, encourage youngsters to take their booklets home to share with family members. With this high-interest activity, reading is in the bag!

CREATIVE DECORATING OPTIONS

- Using yarn, attach a personalized nametag to each bookbag.
- Add colorful stickers to each bookbag.

I put glue in my bookbag.

To extend your back-to-school theme, share the antics of Sarah and her best friend by reading aloud Jack Gantos's *Back to School for Rotten Ralph* (HarperCollins Children's Books, 1998).

Booklet Pattern

Bookbag

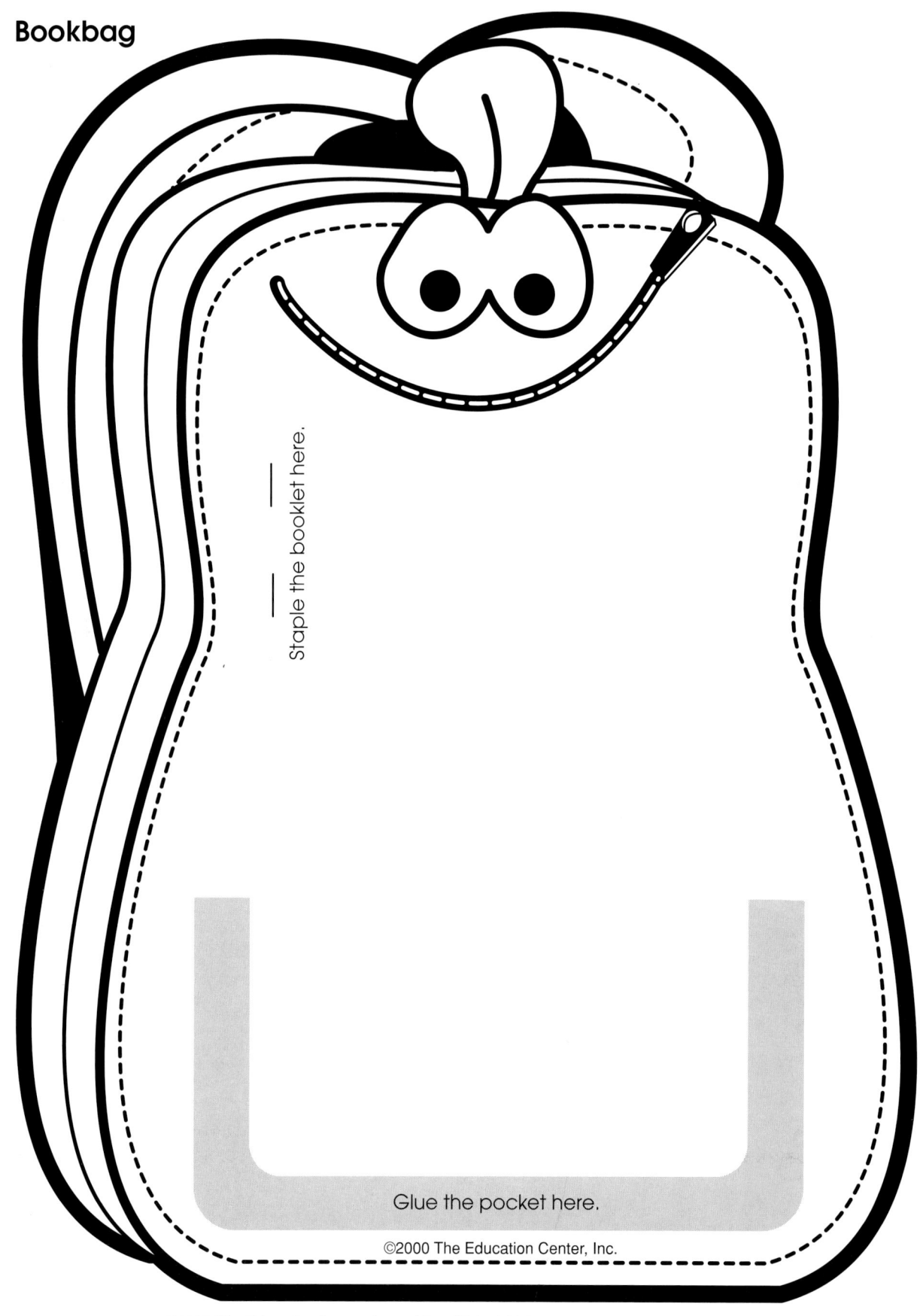

Staple the booklet here.

Glue the pocket here.

©2000 The Education Center, Inc.

Booklet Pages

I put paper in my bookbag. 5	I put glue in my bookbag. 6	I put crayons in my bookbag. 7	I am ready for school. 8

Let's Get Ready for School! 1	_____ Name 2	I have a bookbag. 3	I put a pencil in my bookbag. 4

©2000 The Education Center, Inc. • *I Can Make It! I Can Read It!* • Fall • TEC3509

Note to the teacher: Use with "Let's Get Ready for School!" on page 3.

Booklet Patterns

School Supplies

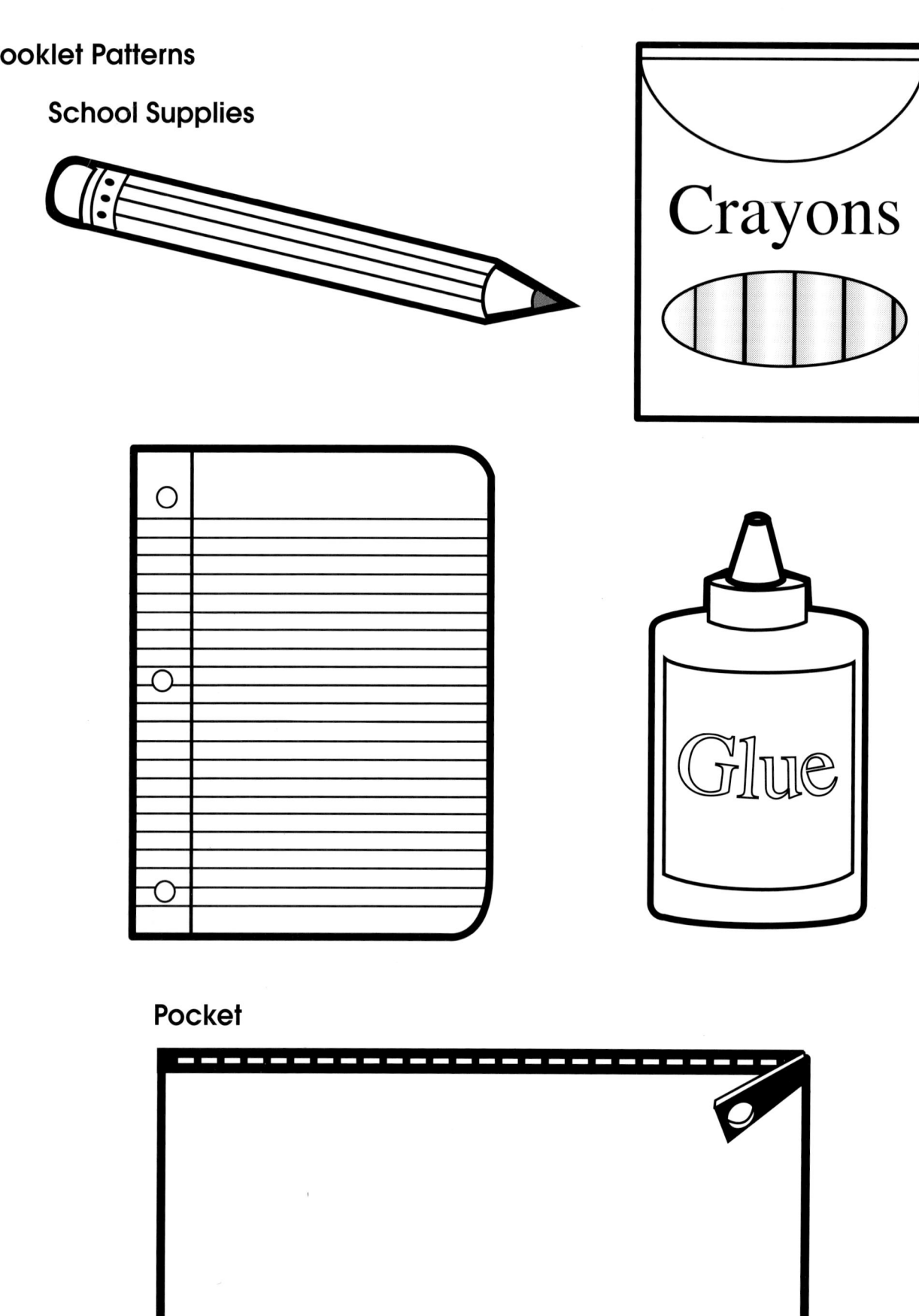

Pocket

©2000 The Education Center, Inc. • *I Can Make It! I Can Read It!* • *Fall* • TEC3509

BINKY RIDES THE BUS!

Students will be ready to roll into reading with this booklet about bus safety! Give each student a copy of pages 8–12. Read the booklet pages with students. Have each student color the cover and booklet pages and then cut them out on the bold outer lines. (Remind students to color lightly over the text so the story can be read.) Next, instruct the student to stack his pages in numerical order, placing the cover on top. Staple each booklet at the top as illustrated. Invite the student to read his completed booklet with a buddy before taking it home to share with family members. All aboard for reading!

CREATIVE DECORATING OPTIONS

- Make copies of the cover on yellow construction paper.
- Glue a photograph of the student on the left-hand window of the school bus cover.

To extend the booklet activity, take Polaroid® group snapshots of your students with their bus drivers. On a copy of the cover on page 8, white-out "Binky Rides." Then make enough yellow construction paper copies for the number of your students' bus drivers. Personalize each cover with "[Bus driver's name] Drives the Bus!" On the back of the cover, glue the appropriate snapshot and have each student write a brief thank-you note to his bus driver. Bus drivers will love the note of appreciation!

Booklet Cover

8 Note to the teacher: Use with "Binky Rides the Bus!" on page 7.

Binky is ready for school. Here comes her bus!

1

A FRIEND TO GROW WITH

Your students' reading abilities are sure to grow with this expanding booklet! Give each student a copy of page 14. Have the student color the treetop, tree trunk, and tree base. (Remind students to lightly color over the text so the booklet can be read.) Instruct him to cut out the patterns on the bold outer lines. Then demonstrate how to carefully cut a slit on the bold lines between each boy's head and the tree. Next, direct him to glue the treetop to the tree trunk and the tree trunk to the tree base where indicated. When the glue is dry, help him accordion-fold the tree trunk on the thin black lines. (Start with the top block, folding it back.)

Then have him carefully tuck the bottom of the treetop into the slits as shown at the left. Be sure to set aside time for youngsters to practice reading with a buddy. Reading with a friend is such a "tree-t"!

CREATIVE DECORATING OPTIONS

- Color birds and squirrels in the treetop.
- Glue a picture of the student and his friend on the treetop.

On large patterns of fall-colored leaves, have students write what it means to be a good friend. Use a hole puncher to make a hole near each leaf's stem. Suspend the leaves with yarn on a four- to five-foot tree branch placed in a large bucket of dirt. Title the display "Friendship to 'Be-leaf' In!"

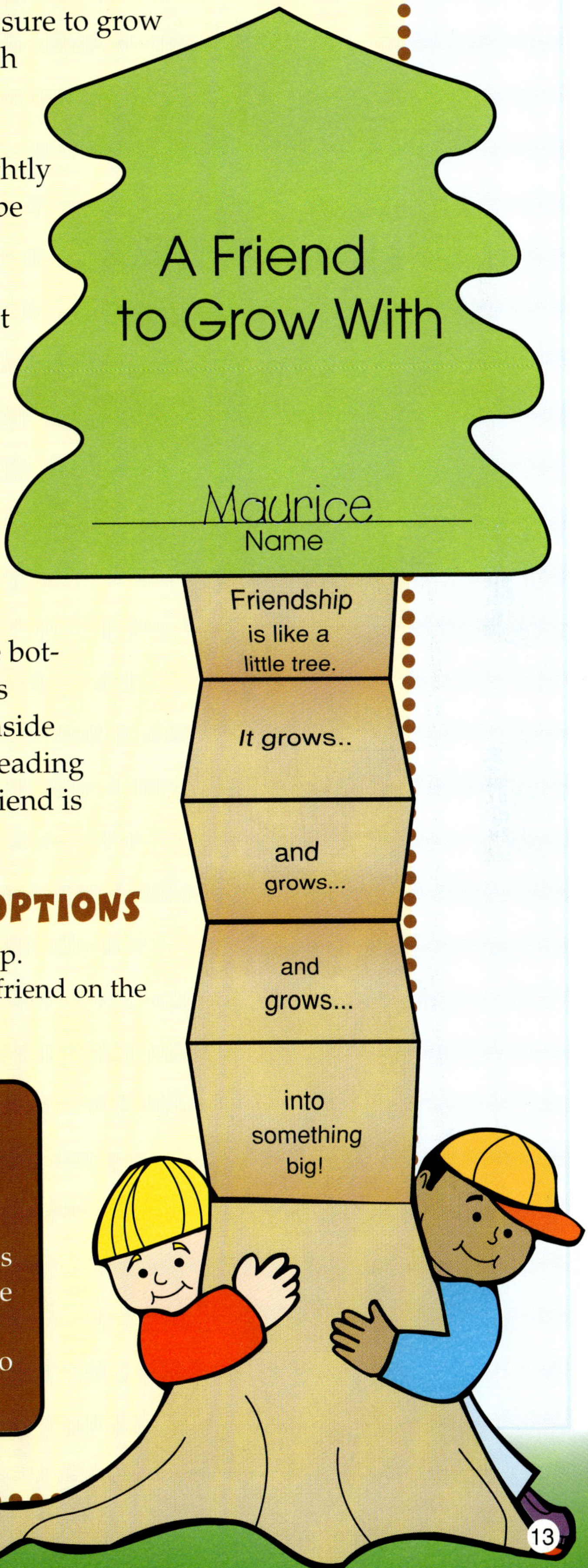

A Friend to Grow With

Maurice
Name

Friendship is like a little tree.

It grows..

and grows...

and grows...

into something big!

Booklet Patterns
Tree Trunk

Treetop

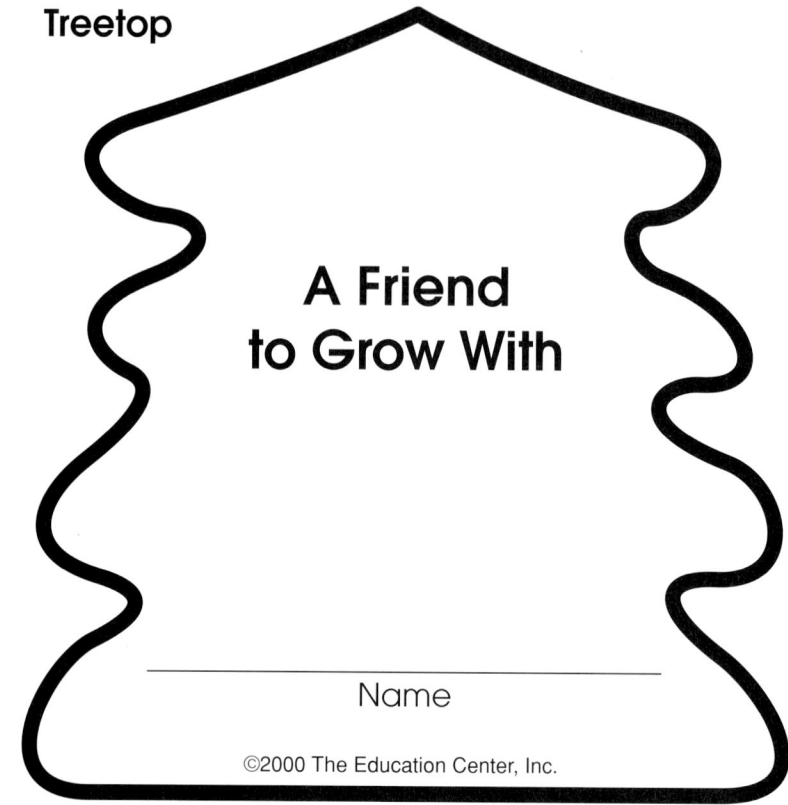

Glue the treetop here.

Friendship is like a little tree.

It grows...

and grows...

and grows...

into something big!

A Friend to Grow With

_____
Name

©2000 The Education Center, Inc.

Tree Base

Glue the tree trunk here.

©2000 The Education Center, Inc. • *I Can Make It! I Can Read It!* • Fall • TEC3509

Note to the teacher: Use with "A Friend to Grow With" on page 13.

ALL ABOUT ME!

Here's a handy way to learn about your students *and* get them reading! Give each student a copy of pages 16–20. Read each booklet page with students. Have each student illustrate her pages according to the text and then cut out the booklet pages on the bold outer lines. (Remind students to color lightly over the text so the story can be read.) Next, explain to students that they are to stack their pages in order according to the time indicated on the watches. When pages are stacked correctly, staple the pages together at the top of the watchband as illustrated. Invite volunteers to read and show their completed booklets to the class. Then, for an open house bulletin board, display each child's booklet beside his self-portrait. Title the display "What Makes Me Tick!"

CREATIVE DECORATING OPTIONS

- Using gold markers and stickers, decorate the cover with rings.
- Use crayons or markers to turn the cover into a colorful glove.

Extend this booklet with a get-to-know-you activity. Have students stand in a circle. Holding a soft rubber ball, stand in the center of the circle. Announce a question, such as "What's your favorite color?" Then toss the ball to a student. Have the student answer the question and toss the ball back to you. Repeat in this manner until each student has answered a question.

Booklet Cover

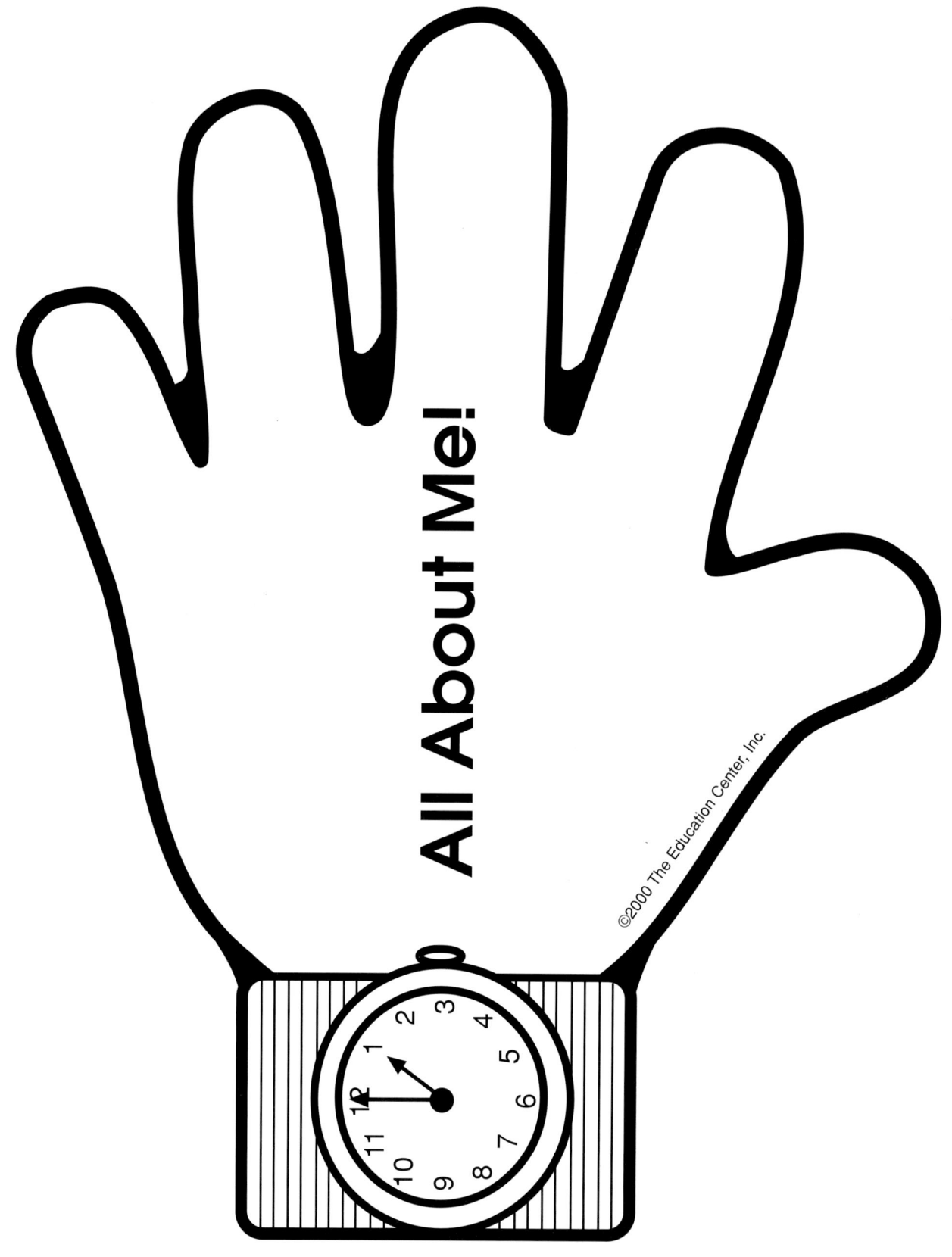

©2000 The Education Center, Inc. • *I Can Make It! I Can Read It!* • Fall • TEC3509

Note to the teacher: Use with "All About Me!" on page 15.

Booklet Page

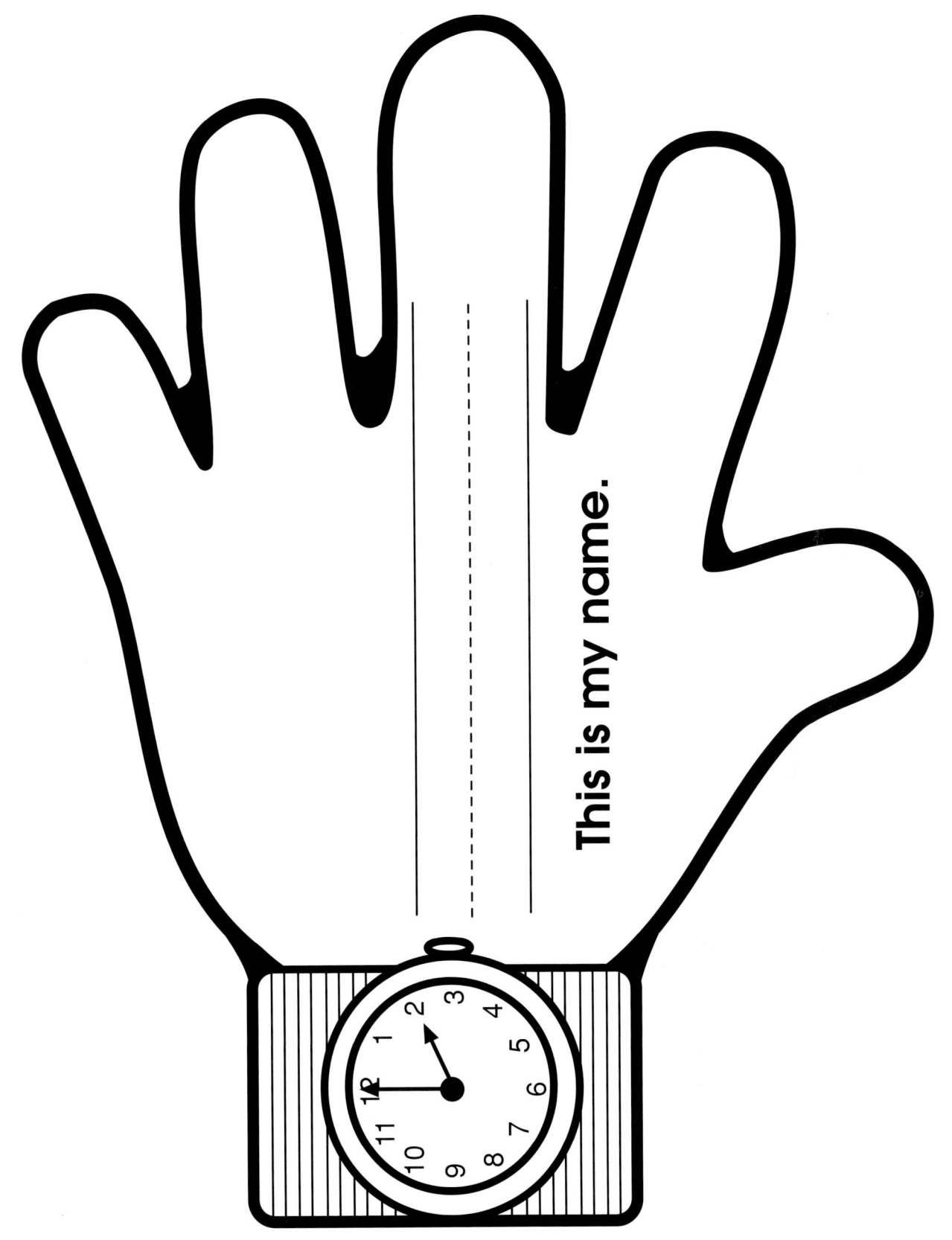

©2000 The Education Center, Inc. • *I Can Make It! I Can Read It!* • Fall • TEC3509

Booklet Page

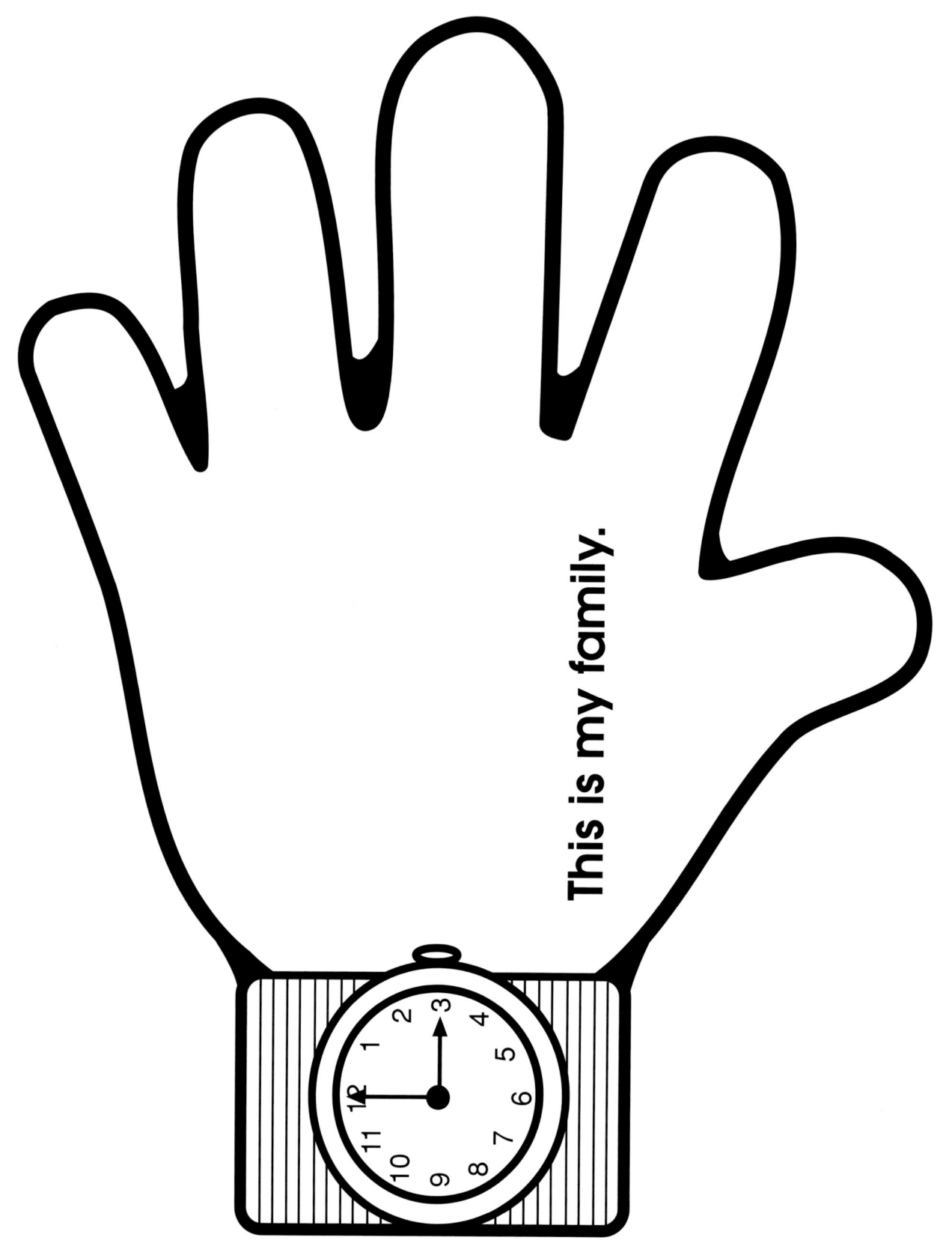

©2000 The Education Center, Inc. • *I Can Make It! I Can Read It!* • *Fall* • TEC3509

Note to the teacher: Use with "All About Me!" on page 15.

Booklet Page

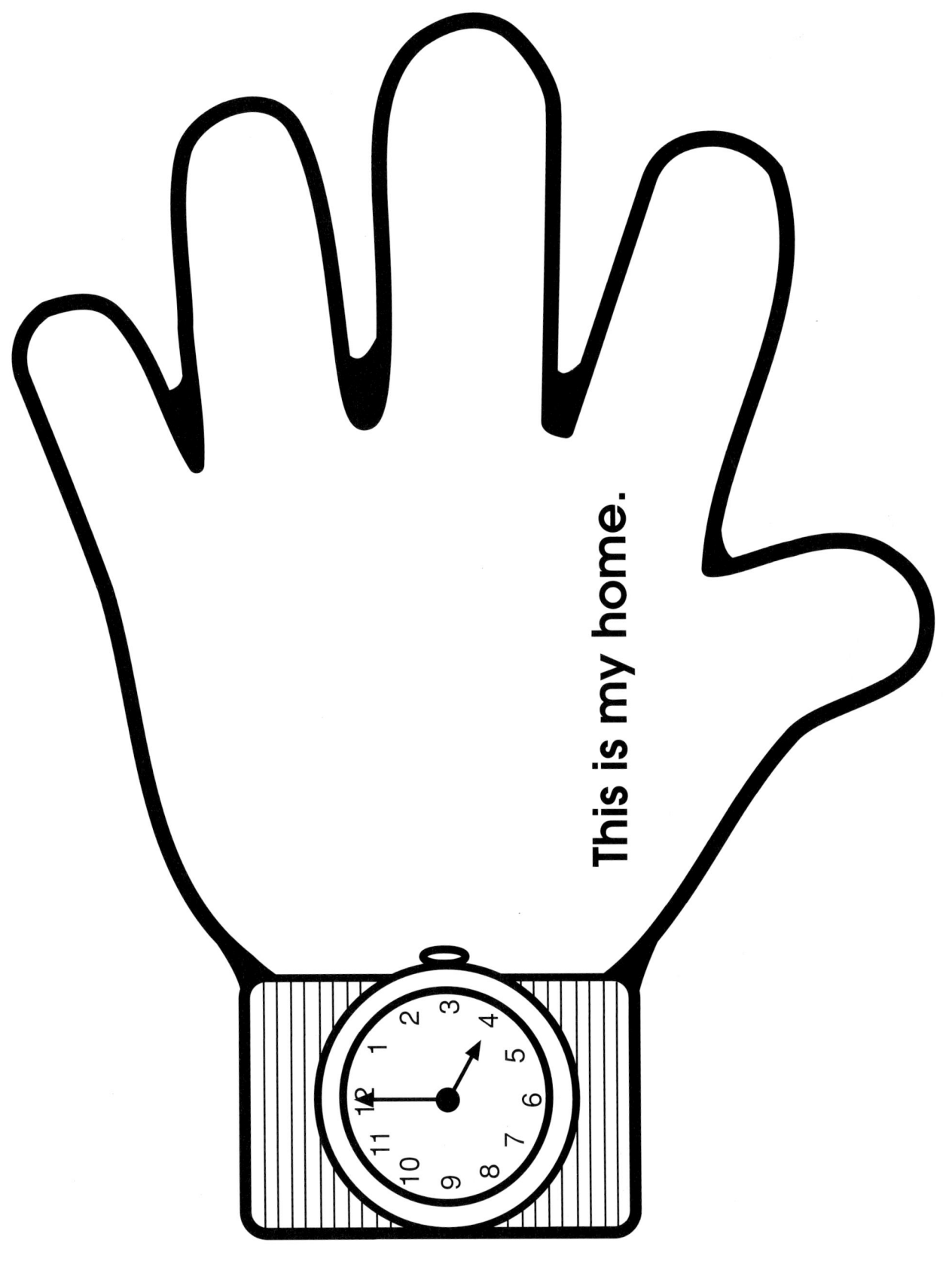

This is my home.

Booklet Page

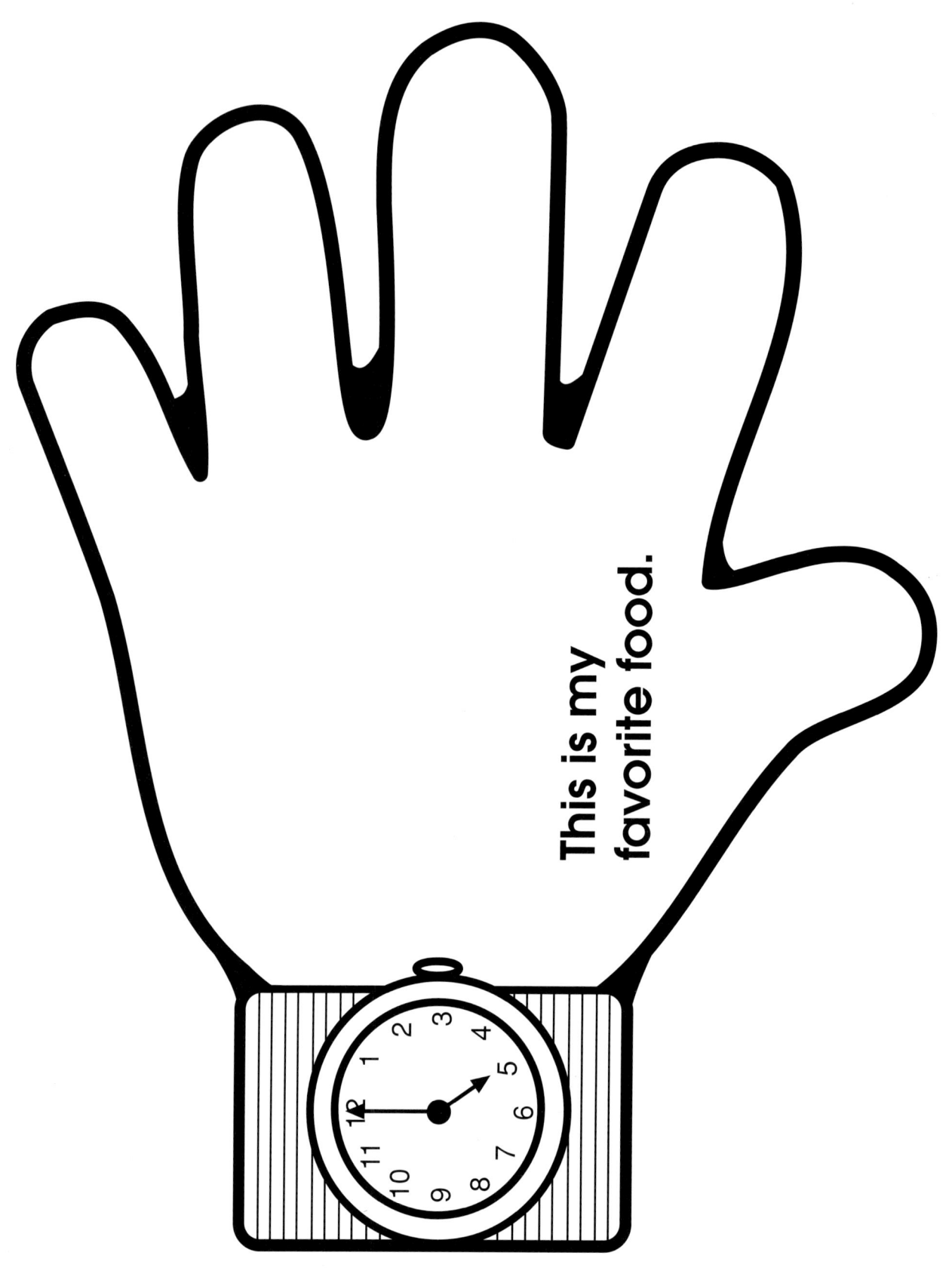

©2000 The Education Center, Inc. • *I Can Make It! I Can Read It!* • *Fall* • TEC3509

Note to the teacher: Use with "All About Me!" on page 15.

WHO HELPS ME?

Rev up reading skills with this unique community helpers booklet! Give each student five six-inch lengths of yarn and a copy of pages 22–24. Read the booklet pages with students. Have each student color her booklet pages and then cut them out on the bold outer lines. (Remind students to color lightly over the text so the story can be read.) Next, instruct the student to hole-punch each vehicle where indicated. Using a length of yarn, have her tie one end to the first vehicle and the other end to the next vehicle. Continue in this manner until all the vehicles are linked together in the correct order. Show students how to accordion-fold their booklet pages, one vehicle behind the next. Encourage each student to read her completed booklet with a buddy. Then invite students to take their booklets home to read to family members. Your youngsters are really going places with reading!

CREATIVE DECORATING OPTION

- Glue a picture of the student in the driver's seat of the first vehicle.

To extend this booklet activity, invite community helpers to talk to students about their work.

Booklet Pages

22 Note to the teacher: Use with "Who Helps Me?" on page 21.

Booklet Pages

Booklet Pages

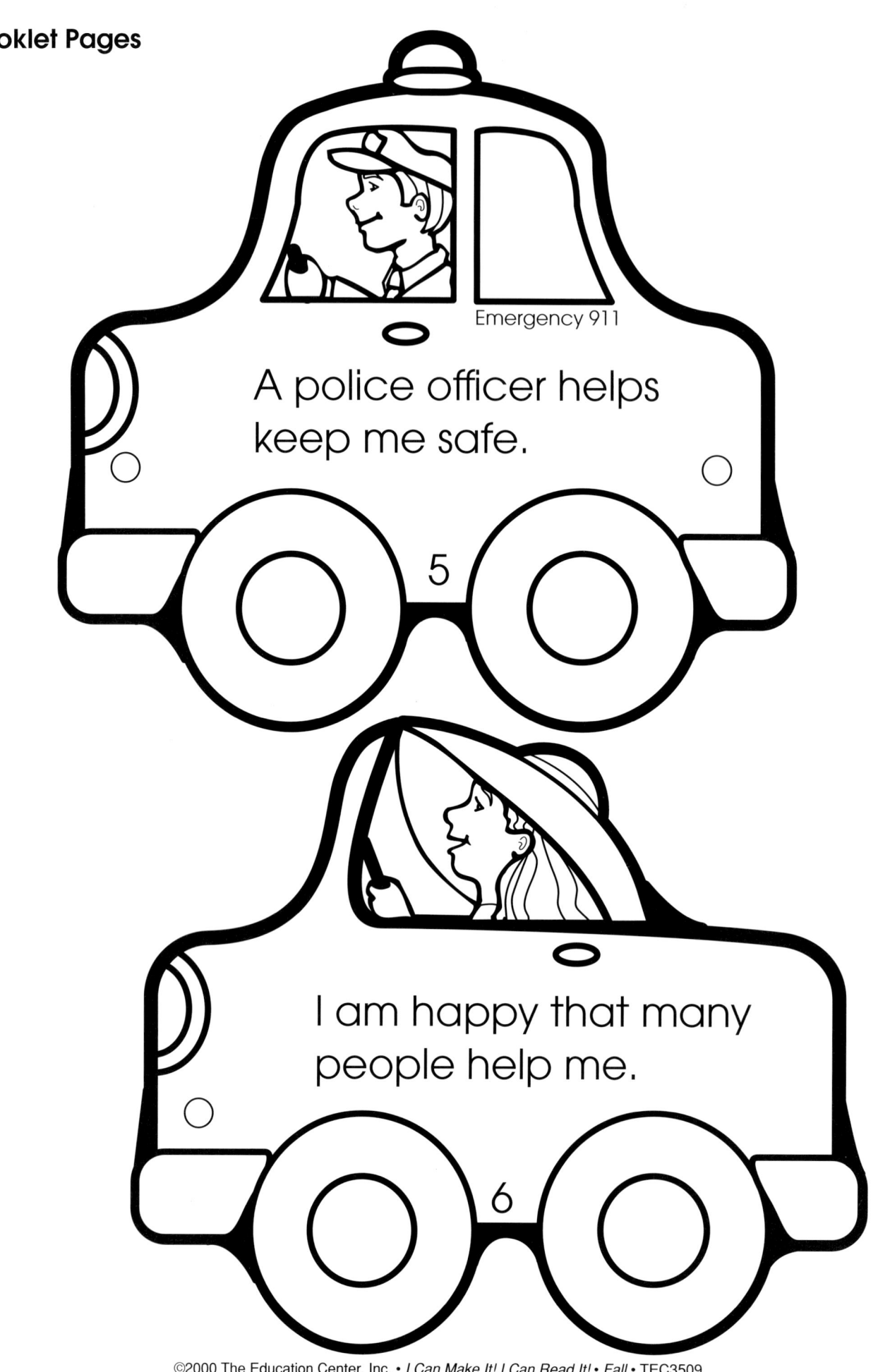

Emergency 911

A police officer helps keep me safe.

5

I am happy that many people help me.

6

©2000 The Education Center, Inc. • *I Can Make It! I Can Read It!* • *Fall* • TEC3509

AROUND MY NEIGHBORHOOD

Strengthen reading skills with this neighborly booklet! Give each student a brad and a copy each of pages 26 and 27. Have the student color the top wheel and then cut out both wheels on the bold outer lines. Next, help him insert the brad through the center holes, first through the top wheel and then the bottom wheel. To read the story, he aligns the top wheel so that the titled paragraph is revealed. After reading the paragraph, he rotates the top wheel in the direction of the arrow and aligns the next paragraph. The student continues in this manner until the four paragraphs have been read. Now that's putting a new spin on reading!

CREATIVE DECORATING OPTIONS

- Use glitter glue to outline the bicycle.
- Have students draw pictures of themselves and their friends riding bikes along the road.

To extend this activity, have each student draw a picture of his neighborhood. Then have him write what he likes best about living there.

Booklet Pattern

Top Wheel

©2000 The Education Center, Inc. • *I Can Make It! I Can Read It!* • Fall • TEC3509

26   **Note to the teacher:** Use with "Around My Neighborhood" on page 25.

THE FOUR SEASONS

Need a booklet to make "seasoned" readers of your youngsters? Use this interactive booklet to reinforce basic vocabulary words and teach about the four seasons! Give students a copy of pages 30–35 and a construction paper copy of page 29. Read booklet pages 1–10 with students. Then direct each student to color the pages that are illustrated. For the pages that have a box, instruct the student to create his own illustration. Next, have him cut out Strips A and B (page 35) on the bold outer lines. Show students how to glue the strips together as indicated. To illustrate the four seasons, have the student color his trees on the strip in the following order: summer, fall, winter, and spring. Next, have him cut out his booklet pages on the bold lines, put them in numerical order, and staple them where indicated on page 29. Then assist students in cutting the slits on page 29. Next, demonstrate for students how to insert the strip through the slits to reveal the first tree. To read the booklet, the student sets it flat on his desk. As he reads about each season, he pulls the strip to reveal the matching tree. Students will be eager to read these special booklets with buddies before taking them home to share with family members.

CREATIVE DECORATING OPTIONS

- Decorate the trees with seasonal objects such as flowers or acorns.
- Use watercolors on the trees to create a colorful effect.

As a writing extension, have each student write a list of things that can be done during each season. Invite the student to illustrate his work.

Booklet Pattern

Note to the teacher: Use with "The Four Seasons" on page 28.

Booklet Pages

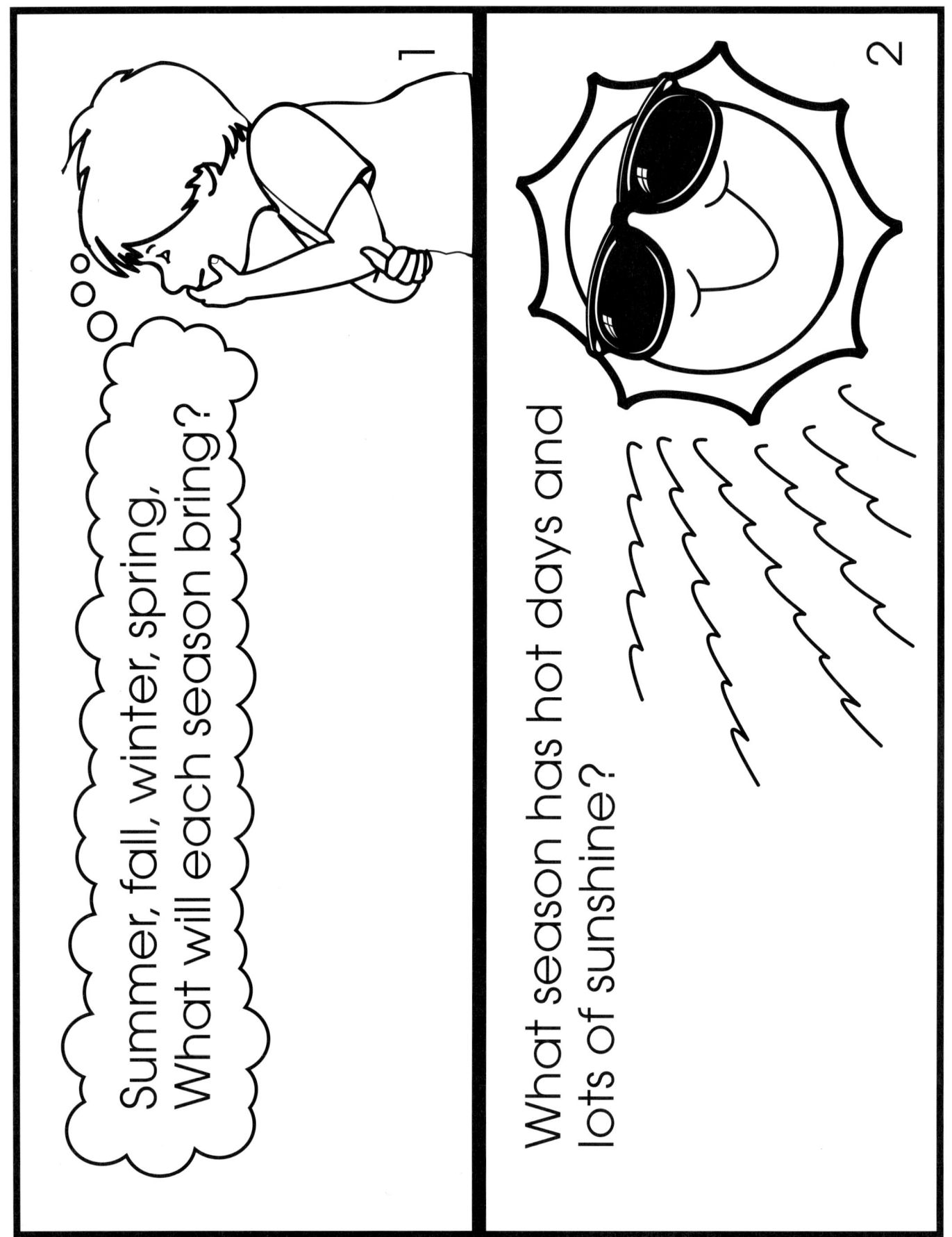

1. Summer, fall, winter, spring. What will each season bring?

2. What season has hot days and lots of sunshine?

Booklet Pages

Summer!
I will go swimming.

3

What season has red, orange, and yellow leaves?

4

Booklet Pages

Fall!
I will jump in the leaves.

5

What season has cold days?

6

©2000 The Education Center, Inc. • *I Can Make It! I Can Read It!* • Fall • TEC3509

32   **Note to the teacher:** Use with "The Four Seasons" on page 28.

Winter!

I will drink hot chocolate.

7

What season has tiny birds hatching from eggs?

8

Booklet Pages

Spring!

9

I will watch mother bird feed her babies.

10

Summer, fall, winter, spring,
Now I know what the seasons bring.
Each season is as fun as can be.
The four seasons are special to me!

Booklet Patterns

Strip A

Strip B

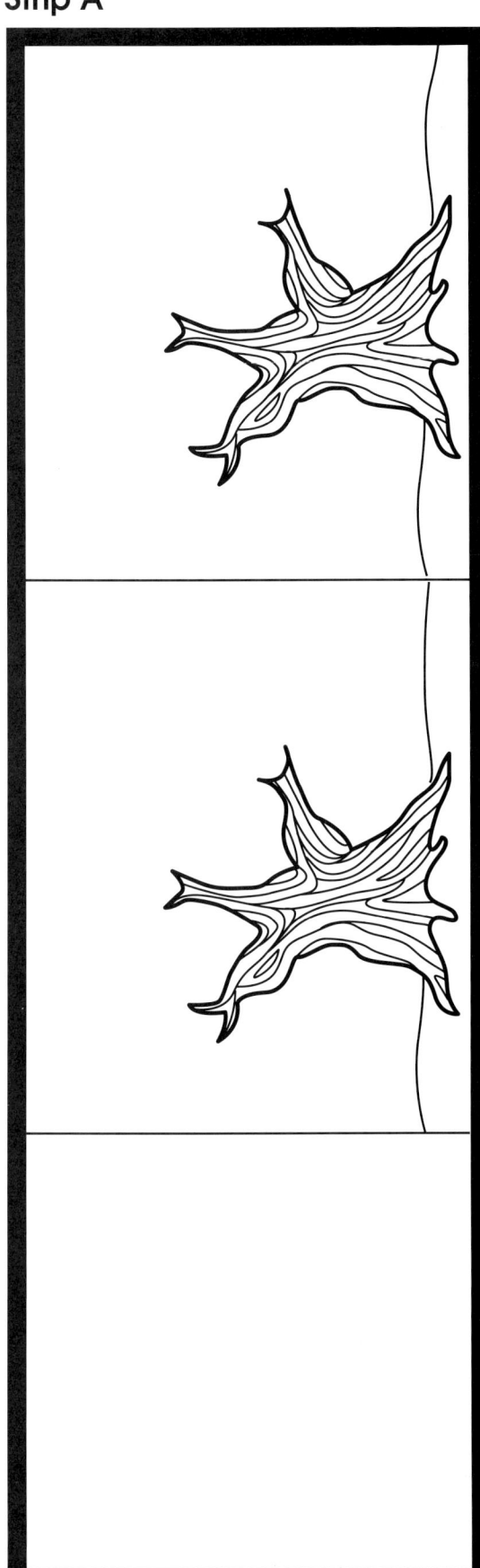

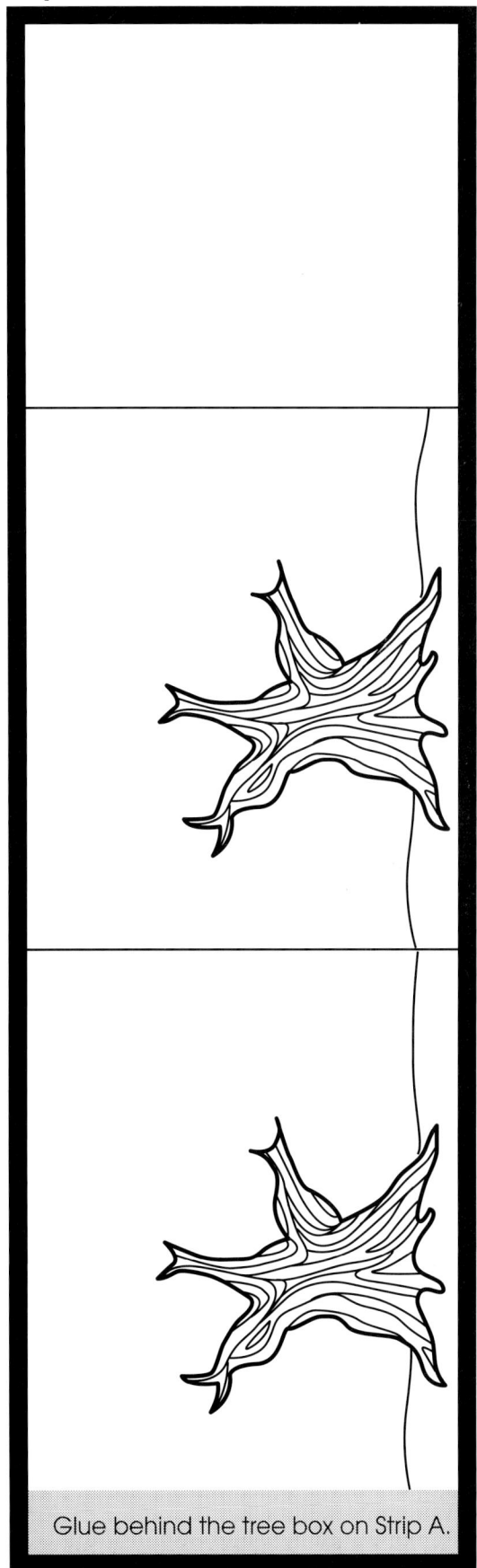

Glue behind the tree box on Strip A.

©2000 The Education Center, Inc. • *I Can Make It! I Can Read It!* • Fall • TEC3509

Note to the teacher: Use with "The Four Seasons" on page 28.

ALL DOLLED UP!

There's something "dress-y" about this months-of-the-year booklet that will get students reading! Ahead of time, prepare a class supply of 7" x 29" strips of bulletin board paper. To make the booklet, give each student a copy of pages 37–41. Demonstrate how to fold back pages 37–39 and carefully cut on the bold outlines to make six paper dolls. Then give each student a strip of bulletin board paper. Help the student glue the paper dolls to the strip as illustrated, keeping the feet flush with the bottom and each paper doll's hands touching the ones beside it. Next, read to students the text on pages 40 and 41. Have students color the articles of clothing, cut them out, and then glue each to its corresponding paper doll. Invite students to add facial features and more clothing to each paper doll. When the glue is dry, show students how to accordion-fold their booklets, starting with the January/February page facing the March/April page. Have the student personalize his cover and title it "All Dolled Up!" Be sure to allow time for each student to read his booklet to a buddy and encourage students to take their booklets home to share. Reading this booklet is designed to be a hit!

CREATIVE DECORATING OPTIONS

- Glue on pieces of scrap yarn to represent hair.
- Using construction paper, add accessories such as sweatbands and earrings.
- Glue a two-inch construction paper star with the student's birthdate to the corresponding booklet page.

To extend this activity, have each student line up for lunch according to his birthday month. For example, announce for children with a January birthday to line up, then those with a February birthday, and so on until all children are in line.

Booklet Pages

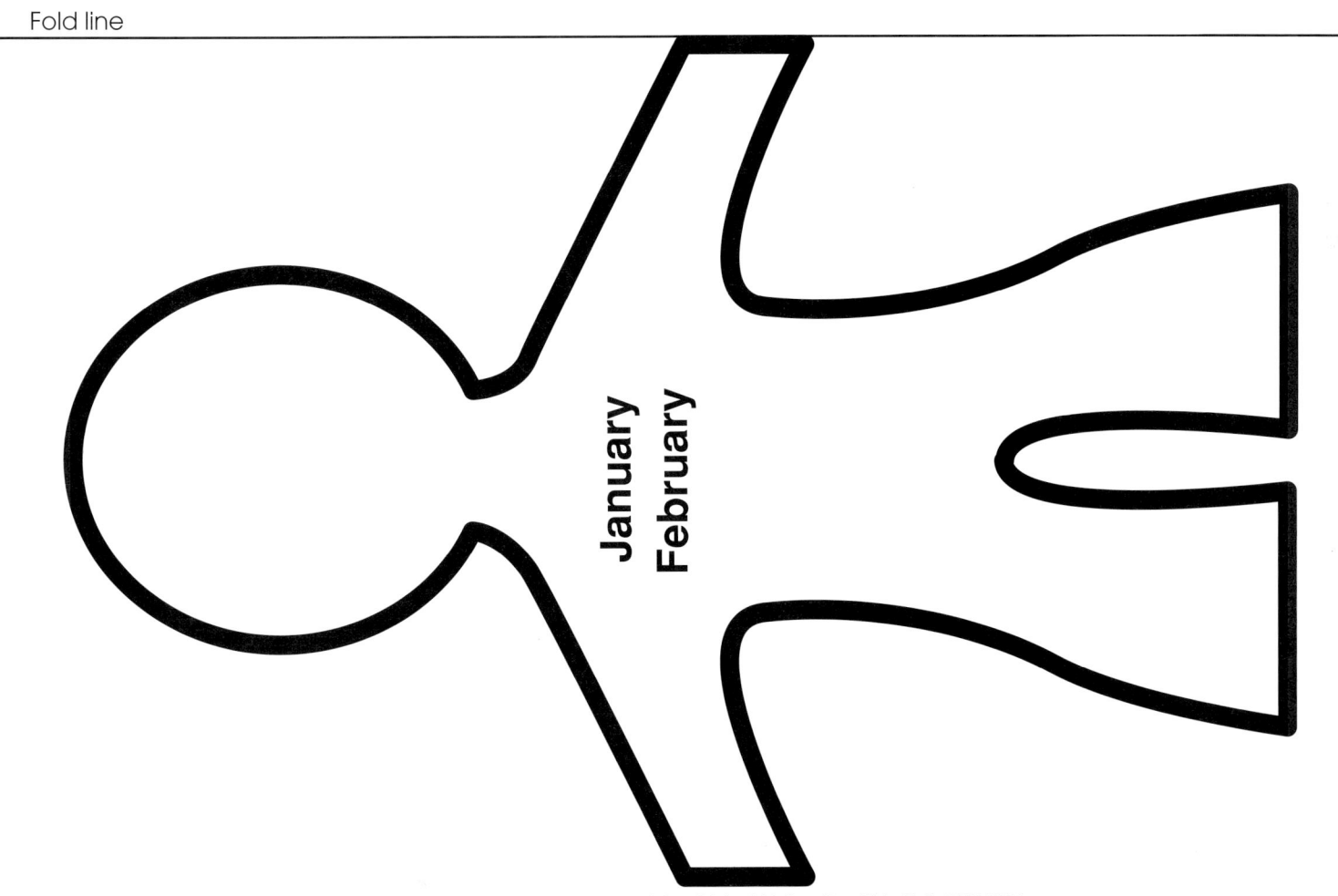

Fold line

Note to the teacher: Use with "All Dolled Up!" on page 36.

Booklet Pages

July
August

Fold line

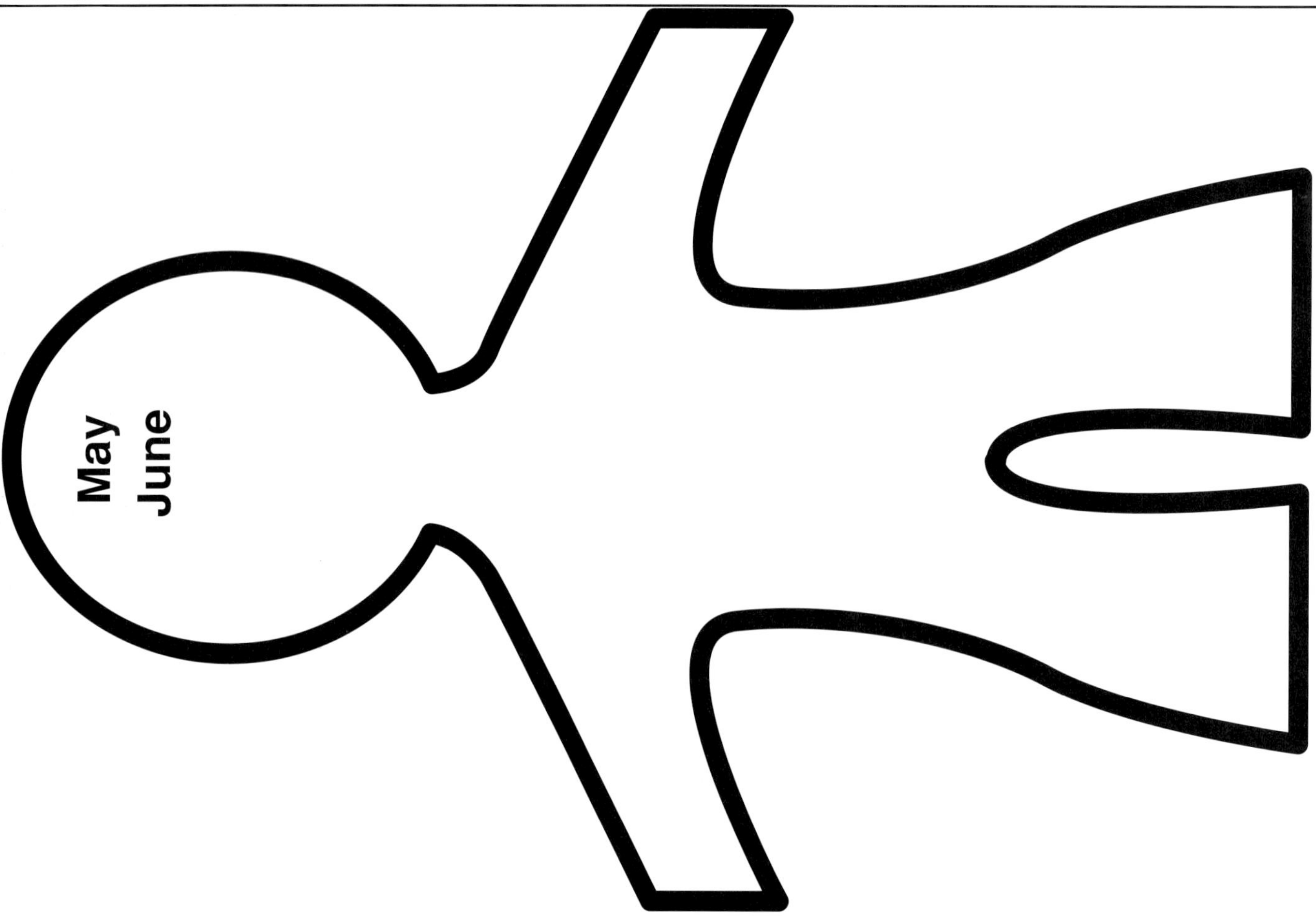

May
June

©2000 The Education Center, Inc. • *I Can Make It! I Can Read It!* • *Fall* • TEC3509

38 **Note to the teacher:** Use with "All Dolled Up!" on page 36.

Booklet Pages

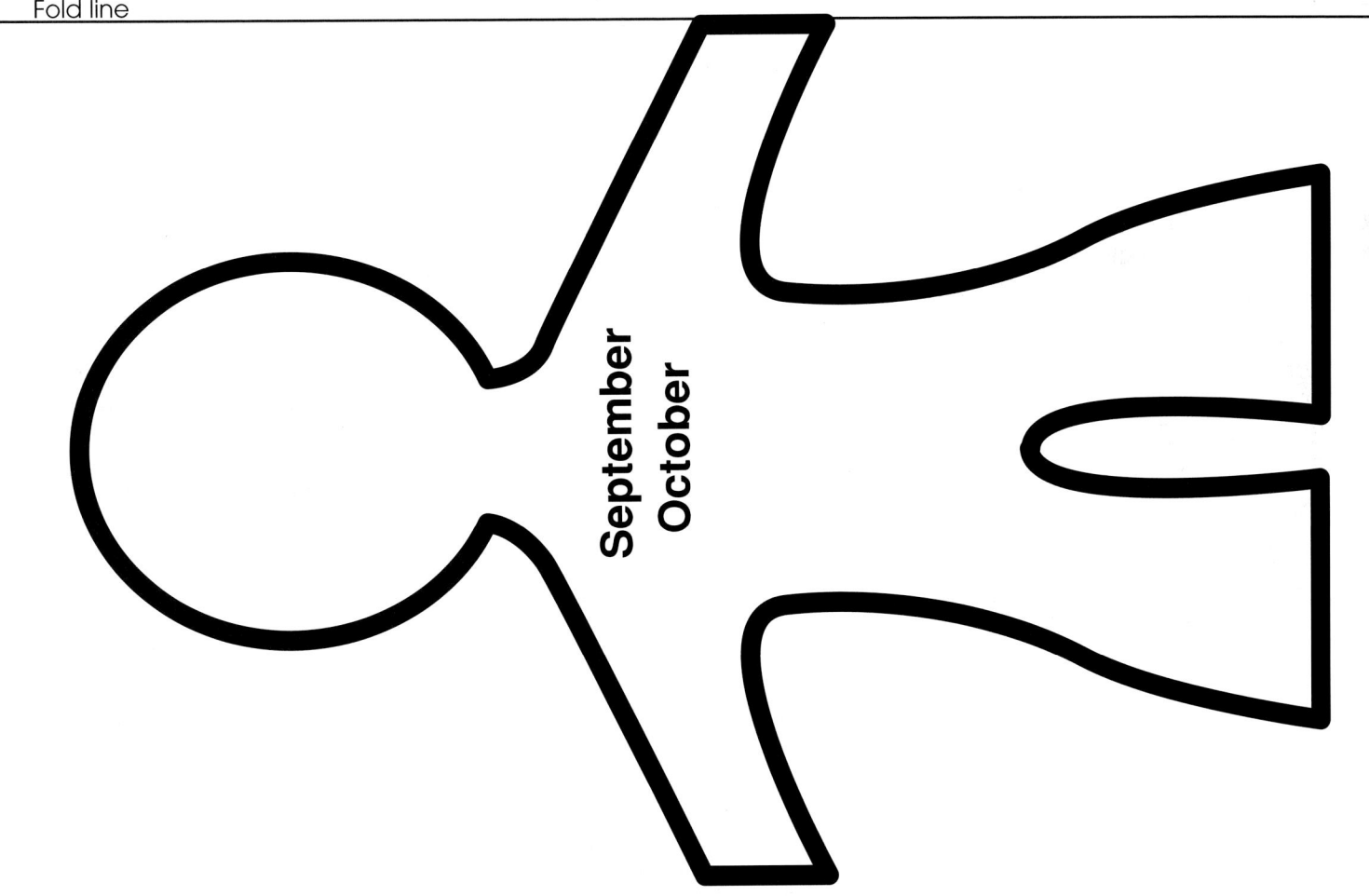

Note to the teacher: Use with "All Dolled Up!" on page 36.

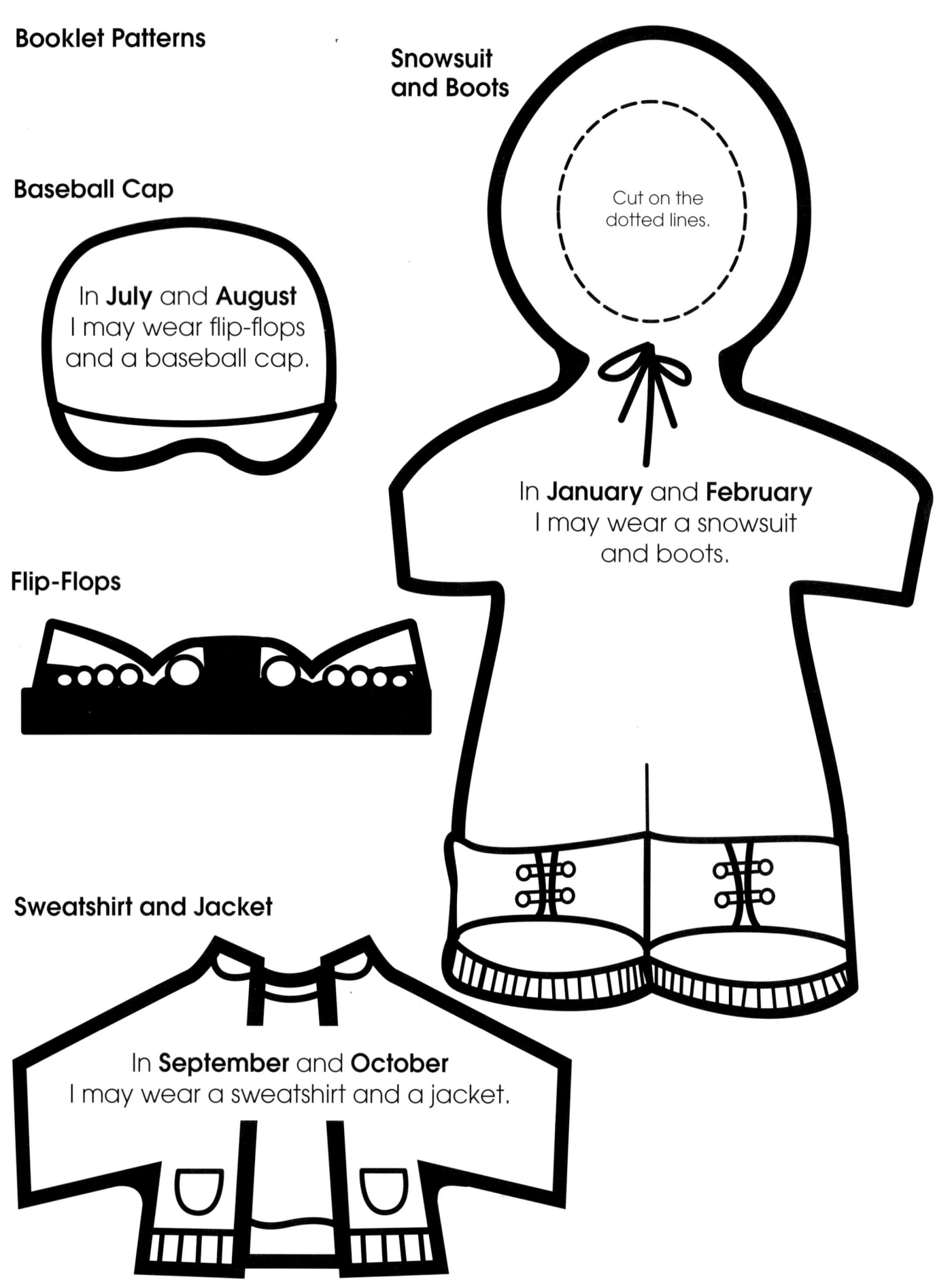

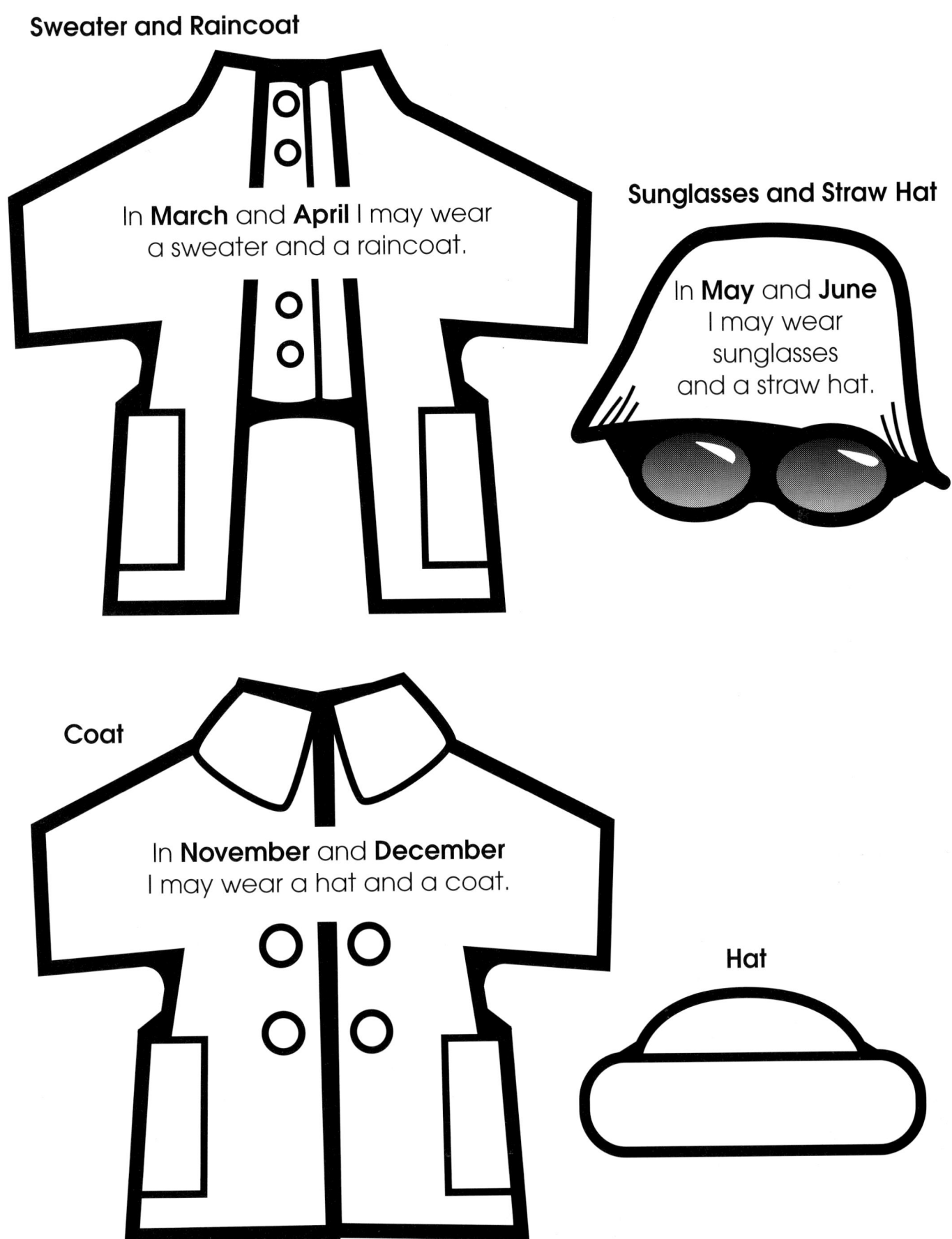

IN THE TREE

Reading will take root with this "tree-mendous" interactive booklet! Give each student a copy of pages 43–45, two sheets of 9" x 6" blue construction paper, and one sheet of 4½" x 6" construction paper in each of the following colors: red, yellow, orange, and brown. Instruct each student to color and cut out her patterns and booklet pages. (Remind students to color lightly over the text so the story can be read.) Then direct the student to glue the animal pictures to the booklet treetops where indicated. On booklet page 4, have her draw a picture of herself in the tree. Next, using the treetop template, have the student trace the shape onto each sheet of 4½" x 6" construction paper and cut out the shapes. Have her align each resulting shape on top of a booklet treetop and then staple it where indicated. Next, have the student glue the cover tree to a sheet of blue construction paper and personalize it. To assemble the booklet, direct her to stack her pages in numerical order and place them between the cover sheets. Staple the top of each student's booklet. Then read a completed booklet with students. Invite the student to practice reading her booklet with a classmate, lifting each treetop to see the answer.

CREATIVE DECORATING OPTIONS

- Glue a picture of the student to the tree on page 4.
- Glue small red, yellow, orange, and brown construction paper leaves to the bases of their matching trees.

To extend this activity, show students what a good friend a tree can be by reading aloud Lois Ehlert's *Red Leaf, Yellow Leaf* (Harcourt Brace Jovanovich, Publishers; 1991).

Booklet Pages

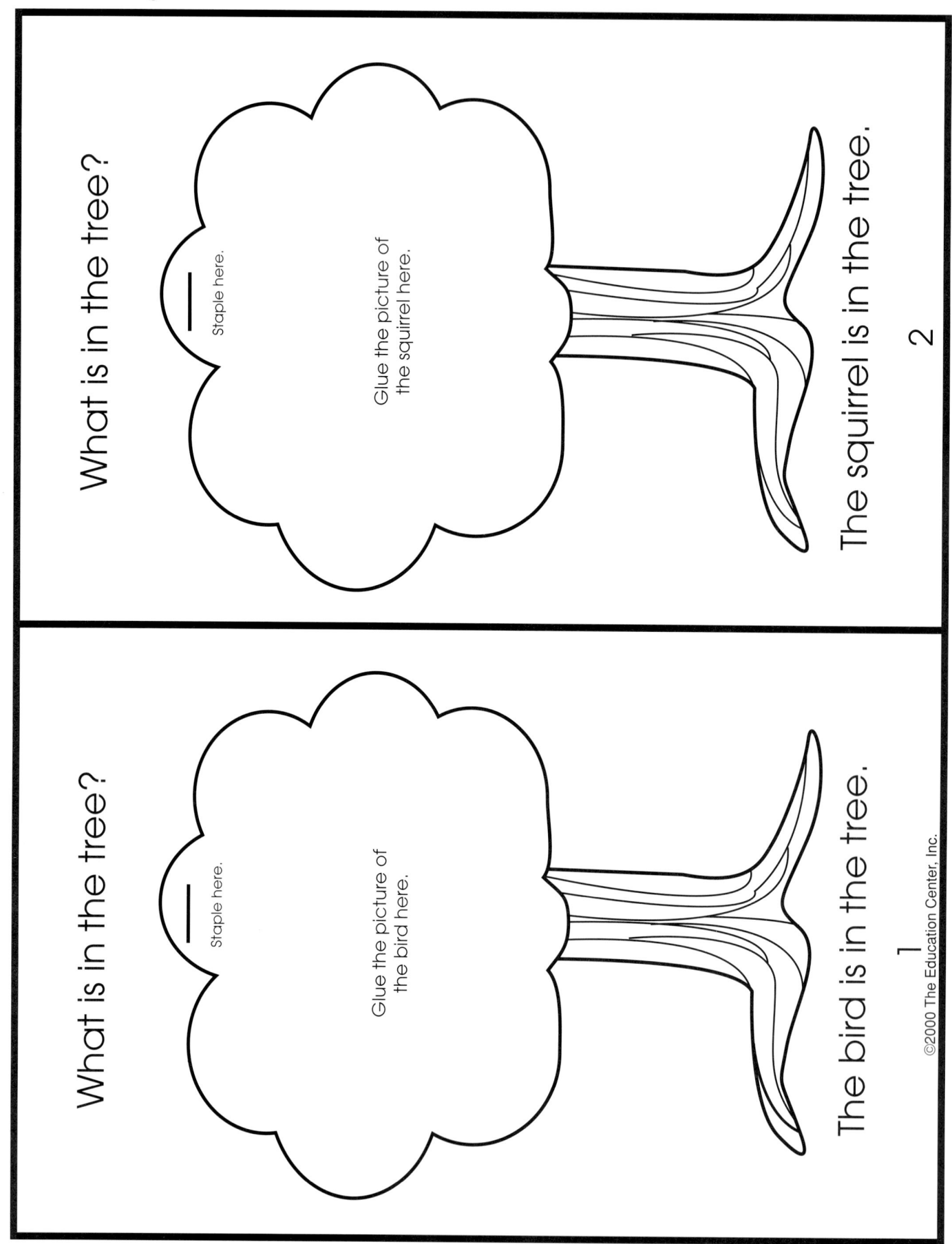

44 **Note to the teacher:** Use with "In the Tree" on page 42.

Booklet Pages

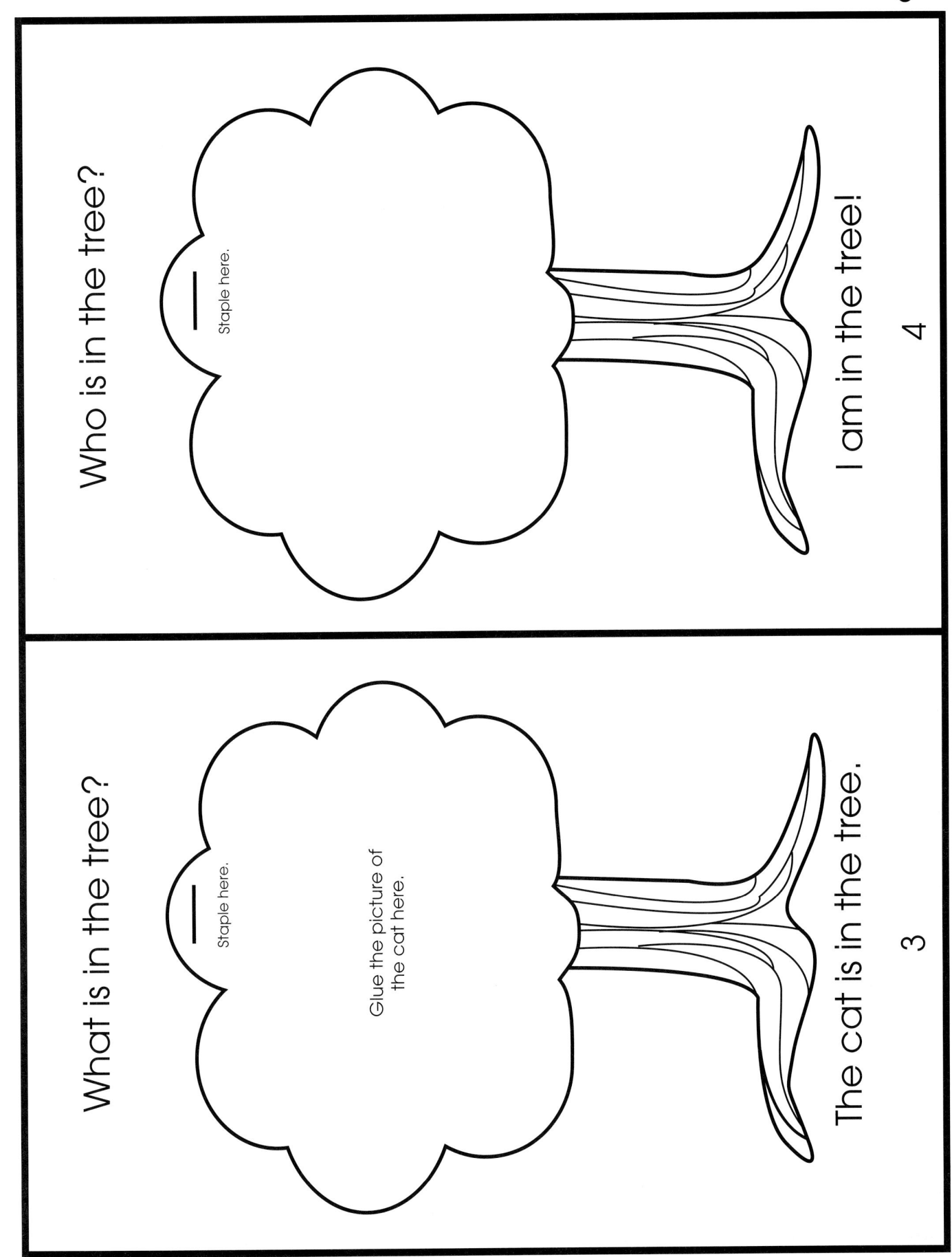

©2000 The Education Center, Inc. • *I Can Make It! I Can Read It!* • *Fall* • TEC3509

Note to the teacher: Use with "In the Tree" on page 42.

A TASTY POEM

This "a-peeling" rhyming booklet is the pick of the crop! Give each student a white construction paper copy of pages 47–49. Ask each student to cut out her booklet cover and pages along the bold lines. Next, have her sequence the cutouts and lay them end to end. Instruct her to glue the cutouts together where indicated to create one long strip (caution students to keep the cutouts in the proper order). Read the poem with students; then have each youngster personalize her cover and illustrate the pages as desired. Using the fine lines as guides, help each student accordion-fold the pages as shown. Have each youngster practice reading her completed booklet; then encourage her to take it home to read with family members. What a great way to provide bushels of reading practice!

CREATIVE DECORATING OPTIONS

- Illustrate the apples by making fingerprints with red, yellow, and green paint.
- Use glue and scraps of colored construction paper to illustrate the pages.
- To represent the inchworm, glue a short length of green yarn onto each page.
- Use a green crayon to outline the inchworm segment on each page.

Extend this booklet-making activity by reading with students the award-winning picture book *Inch by Inch* by Leo Lionni (Mulberry Books, 1995).

Booklet Cover and Pages

Booklet Pages

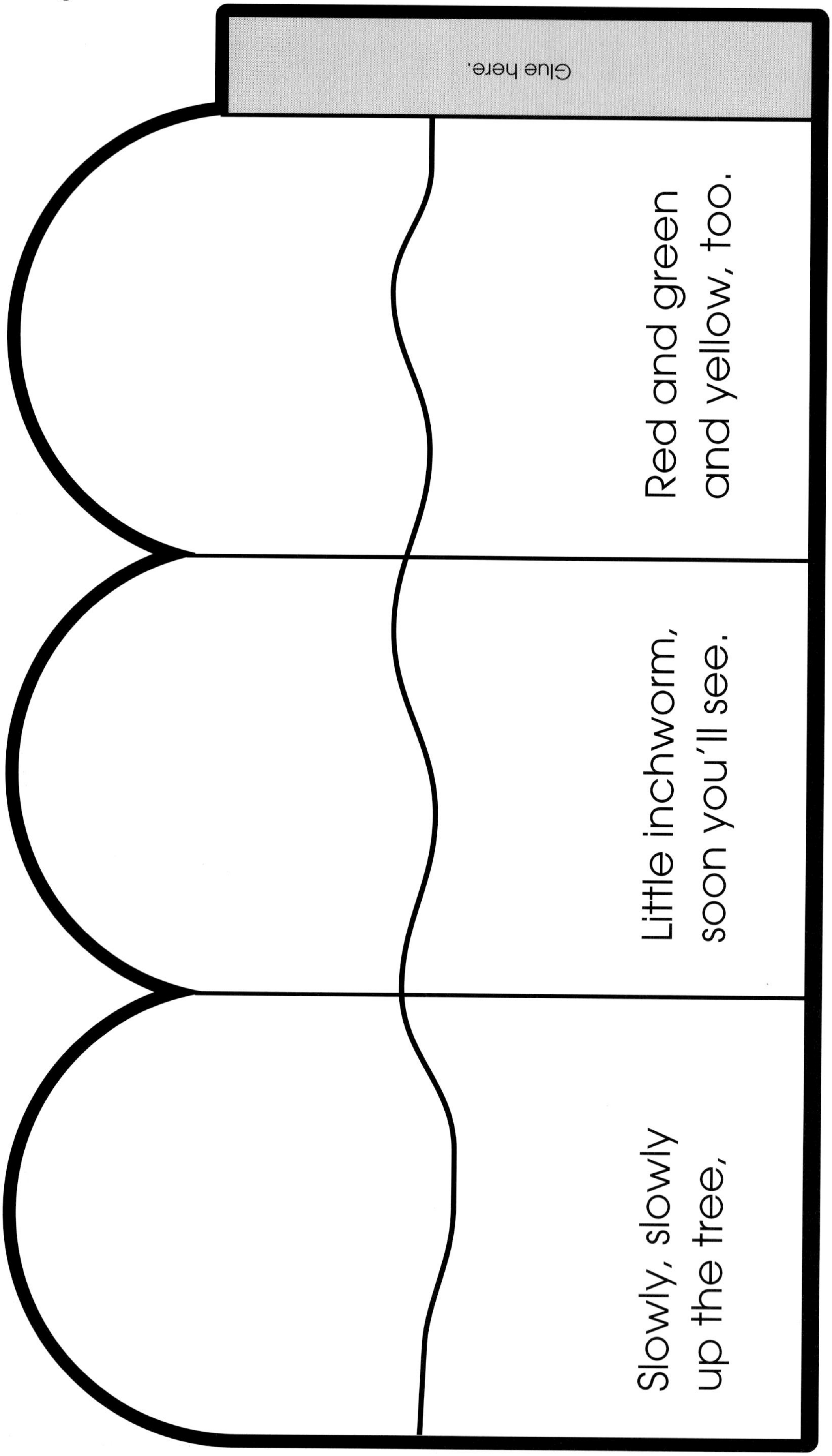

Glue here.

Red and green and yellow, too.

Little inchworm, soon you'll see.

Slowly, slowly up the tree,

©2000 The Education Center, Inc. • *I Can Make It! I Can Read It!* • Fall • TEC3509

Note to the teacher: Use with "A Tasty Poem" on page 46.

Booklet Pages

Yum!

Tasty apples just for you!

©2000 The Education Center, Inc. • *I Can Make It! I Can Read It!* • Fall • TEC3509

Note to the teacher: Use with "A Tasty Poem" on page 46.

DALMATIAN DOLLY'S SAFETY RULES

Here's a fire safety booklet that's not *too* hot for your readers to handle! Give each student a copy of pages 51–53. Read the text on pages 52 and 53 aloud. Then have each student color Dalmatian Dolly and the cover. Instruct the student to cut out the patterns and booklet pages on the bold outer lines. Next, direct the student to stack her booklet pages (not the cover) in numerical order, placing the title page on top. Then have her staple the booklet pages to the left-hand side of Dalmatian Dolly and the cover to the right-hand side as shown. Encourage students to practice reading their booklets with buddies before taking them home to read to family members. What a fun way to ignite reading interest!

CREATIVE DECORATING OPTIONS

- Glue a construction paper fire hydrant to the left side of Dalmatian Dolly.
- Glue glitter to the water coming out of the fire hose.

Extend this booklet by inviting a firefighter to visit your classroom to discuss fire safety.

Dalmatian Dolly

Booklet Pattern

©2000 The Education Center, Inc. • *I Can Make It! I Can Read It!* • Fall • TEC3509

Note to the teacher: Use with "Dalmatian Dolly's Safety Rules" on page 50.

Booklet Pages and Cover

Cover

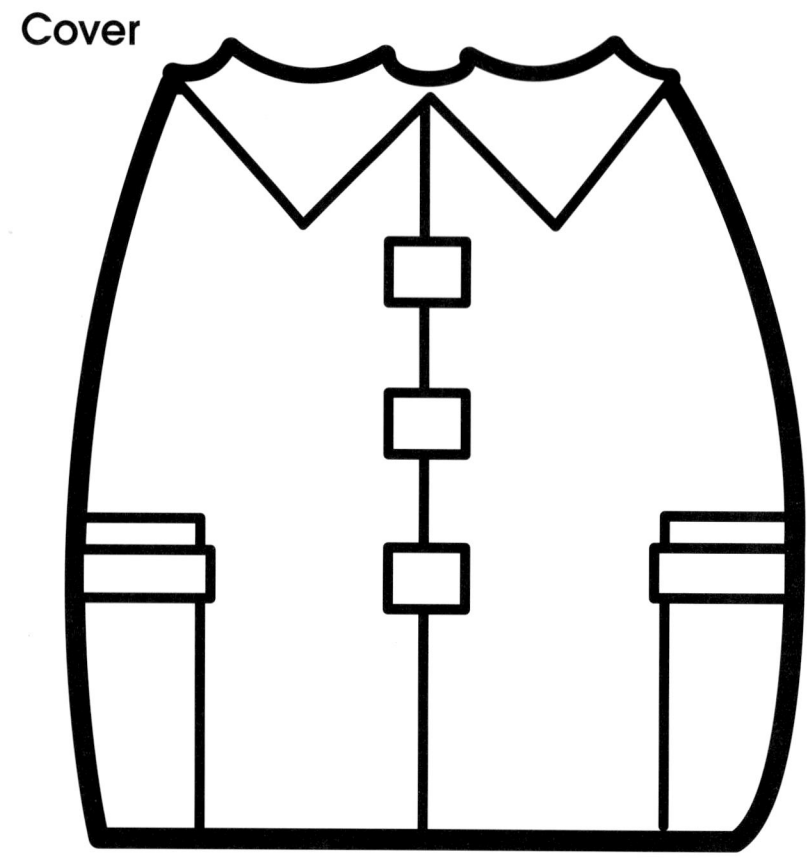

Title Page

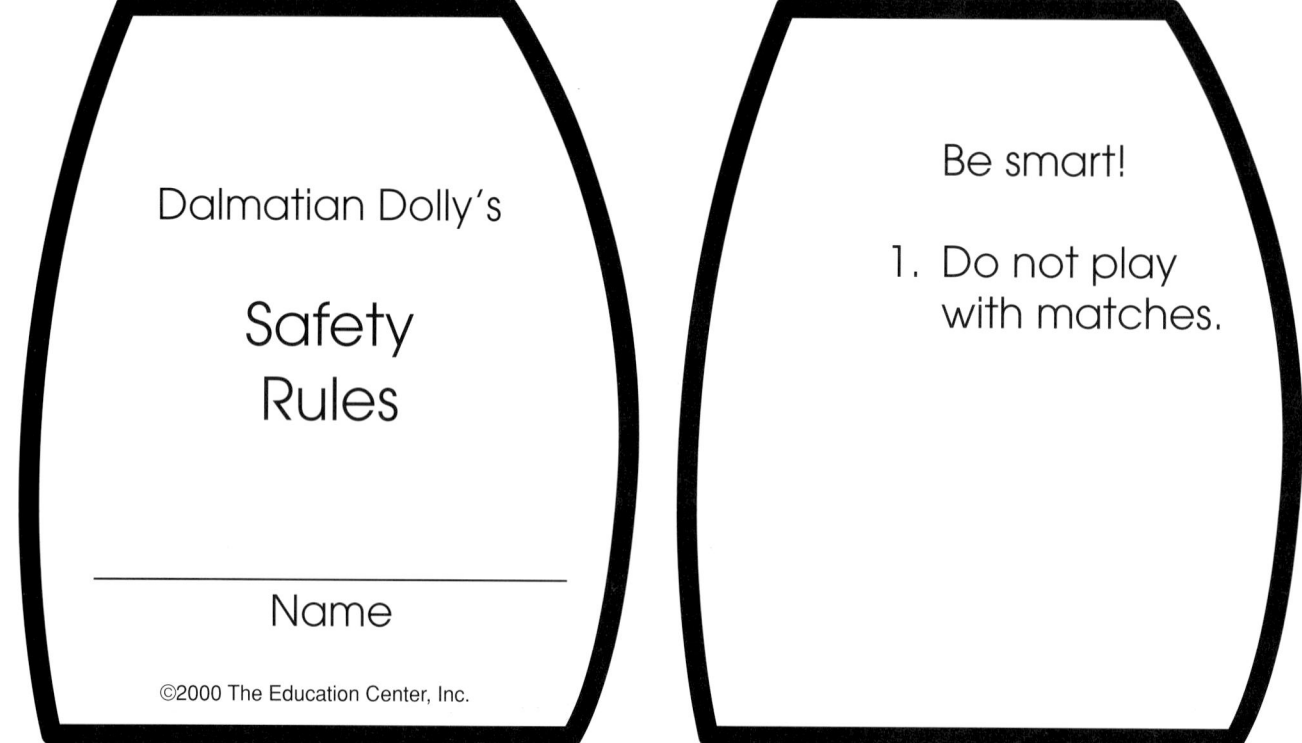

Dalmatian Dolly's

Safety Rules

_____
Name

©2000 The Education Center, Inc.

Be smart!

1. Do not play with matches.

2. Do not play with the stove.

3. If your clothes catch on fire, remember to

Stop!

Drop!

Roll!

4. Tell an adult if you smell smoke.

5. If there is a fire, get out fast!

Remember these rules, and you'll be smart about fire safety!

Note to the teacher: Use with "Dalmatian Dolly's Safety Rules" on page 50.

MR. OWL

Use this rhyming booklet to read "owl" about it! Give each student a copy of pages 56–58 and a brown construction paper copy of page 55. Instruct each student to cut out the booklet pattern and booklet pages on the bold lines. Next, have the student color and fold the beak and then glue it centered below Mr. Owl's eyes. Have students stack their pages in order (the cover on top, then the title page, followed by the booklet pages in numerical order). Place the stack in the center of the brown construction paper owl and staple where indicated. Next, show students how to fold the wings on the dotted lines so that they overlap the cover. Invite students to color feathers on the outside of the folded wings and to color Mr. Owl's face. Read with students their completed booklets. Youngsters will have a hootin' good time reading this booklet to friends and family!

CREATIVE DECORATING OPTIONS

- Use elbow macaroni and liquid tempera paint to print feather patterns on the outside of the folded wings.
- Punch a hole in the top center of the owl. Use yarn to suspend the booklets from a large tree made of bulletin board paper.

What goes bump in the night? It's a fuzzy owl! Read to students the heartwarming picture book *Hoot* by Jane Hissey (Random House, Inc.; 1997).

Booklet Pattern

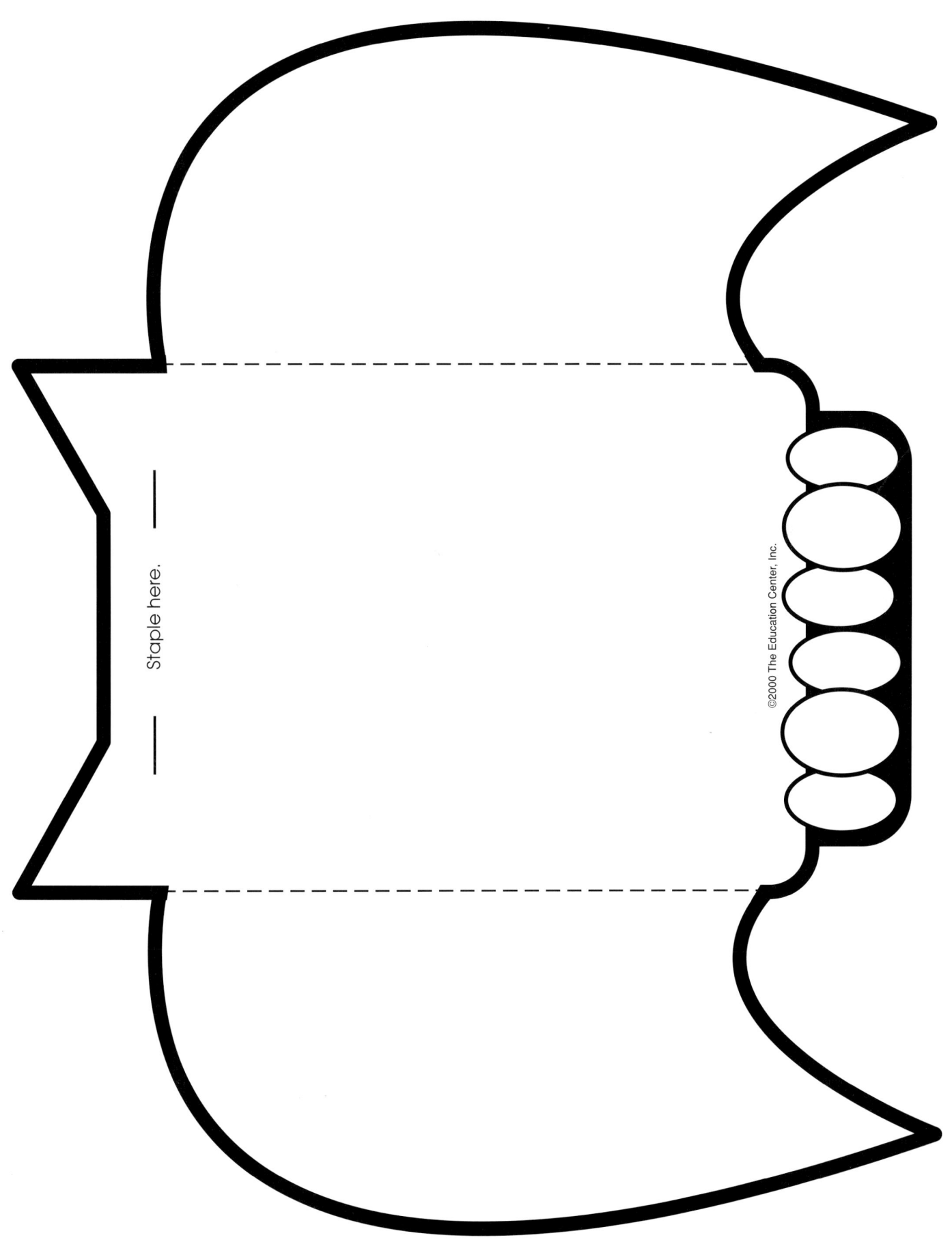

Booklet Pages and Cover

Cover

Title Page

Beak

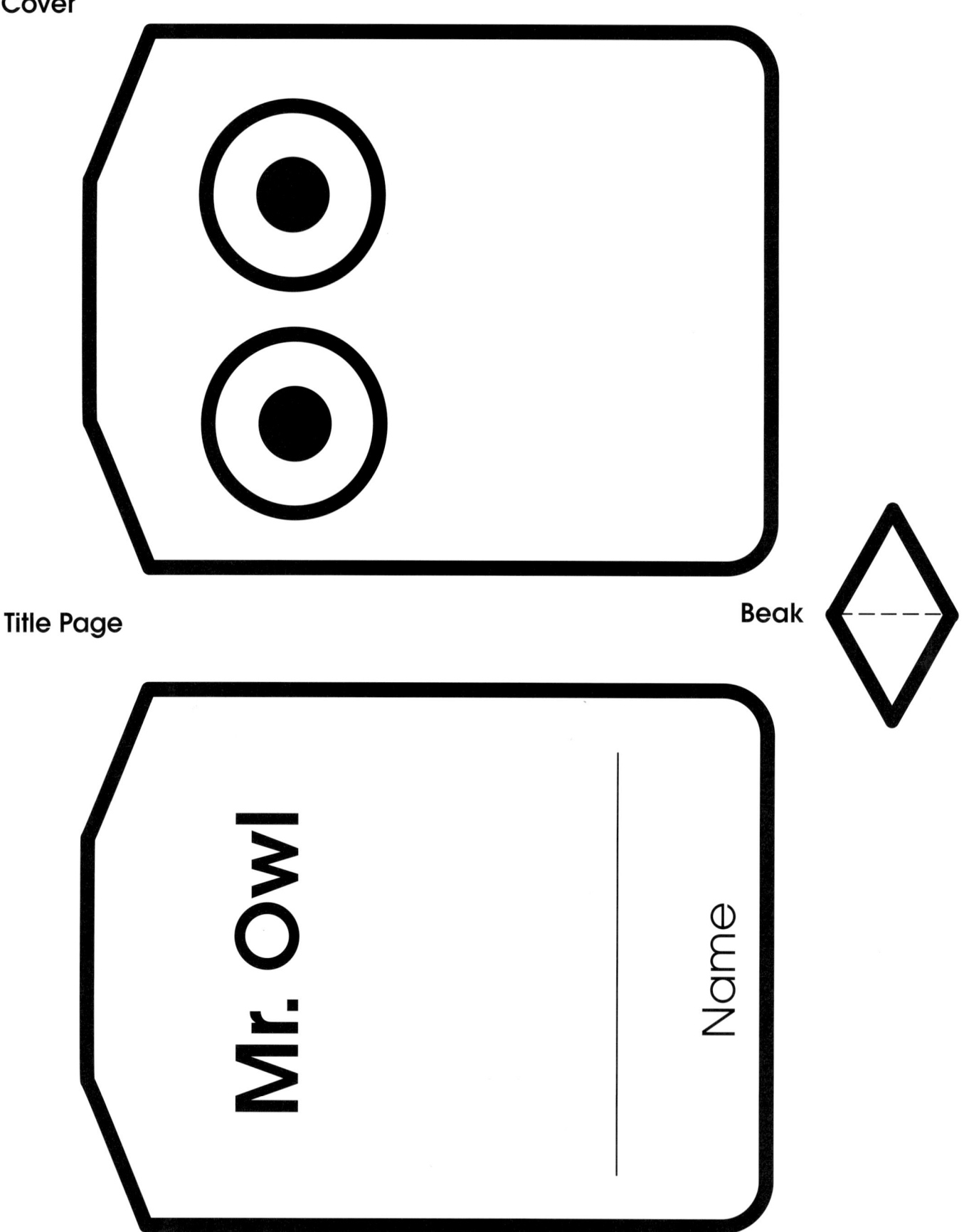

©2000 The Education Center, Inc. • *I Can Make It! I Can Read It!* • Fall • TEC3509

Note to the teacher: Use with "Mr. Owl" on page 54.

Said Mr. Owl, up in a tree,

1

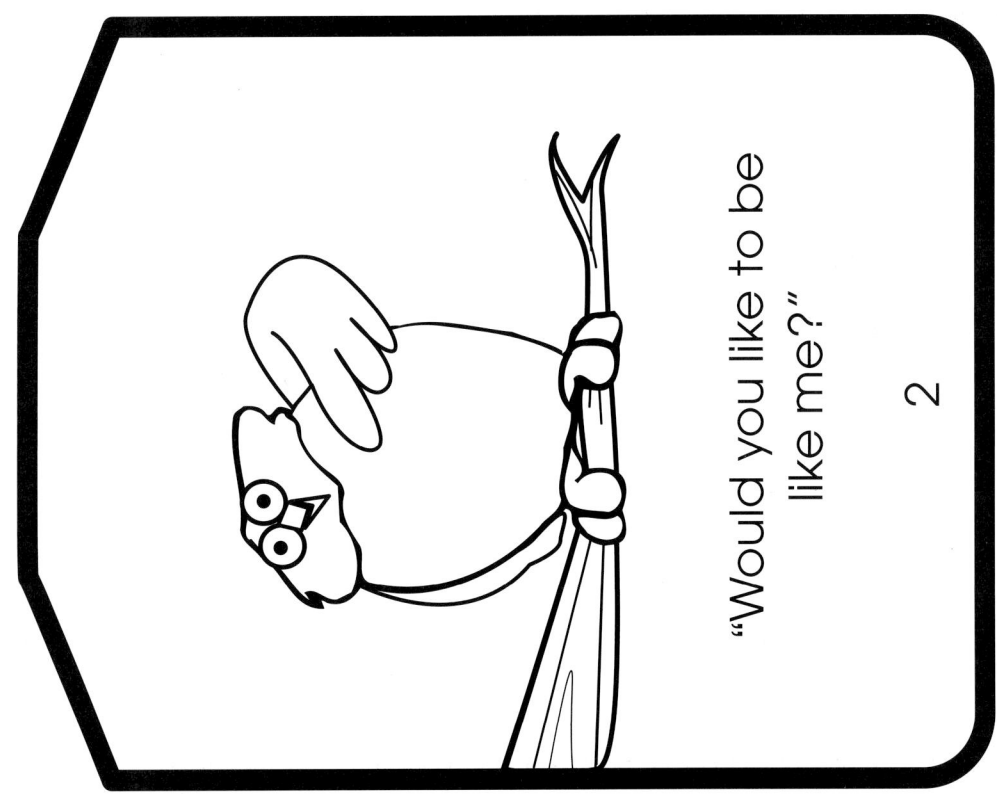

"Would you like to be like me?"

2

Booklet Pages

"I sleep all day in the warm sunlight,

3

and look for food in the black, black night."

4

LET'S GO BATTY!

Spark your youngsters' interest in reading with this "bat-acular" interactive booklet! Give each student a copy of pages 60–63. Read the booklet pages with students. On booklet page 7, have each student read the question and program her answer in the tab on the wing. Instruct her to color her booklet pages. (Remind her to color lightly over the text so the booklet can be read.) Then have her cut out the booklet pages on the bold outer lines and fold back each answer tab along its wing or branch. Next, have her stack the pages in numerical order, placing the cover on top. Staple each booklet along the edge of the left wing. Demonstrate how to read a question and then flip the tab to show the answer. Then provide time for each student to practice reading her completed booklet with a classmate. Encourage students to take their booklets home to read to family members. There is no "bat-ter" way to practice reading!

CREATIVE DECORATING OPTION
- Glue wiggle eyes to the bat on the cover.

Extend this booklet-making activity by reading and talking about the interesting bat facts in the delightful book *Stellaluna* by Janell Cannon (Harcourt Brace & Company, 1993).

Booklet Pages and Cover

Cover

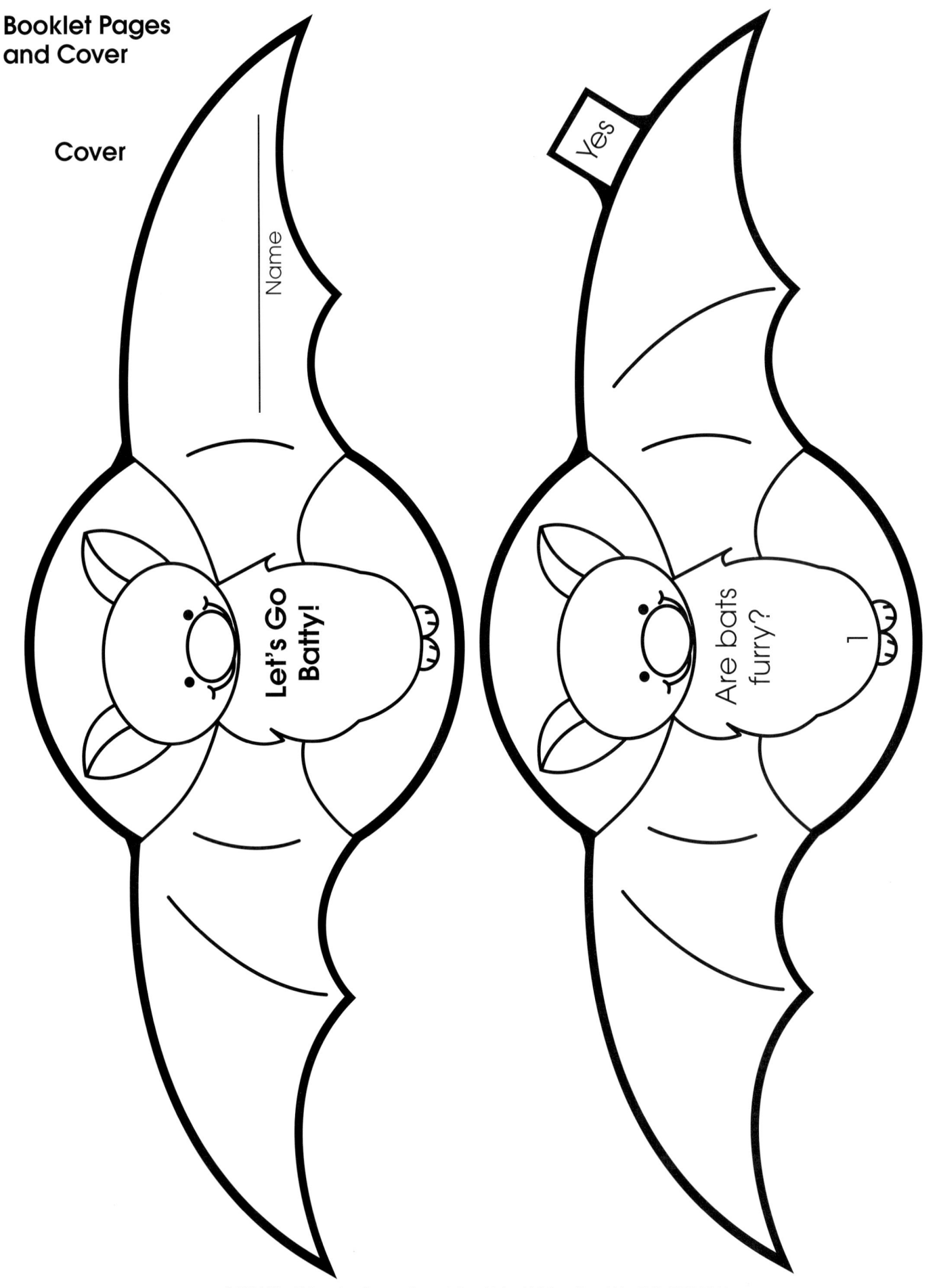

Booklet Pages

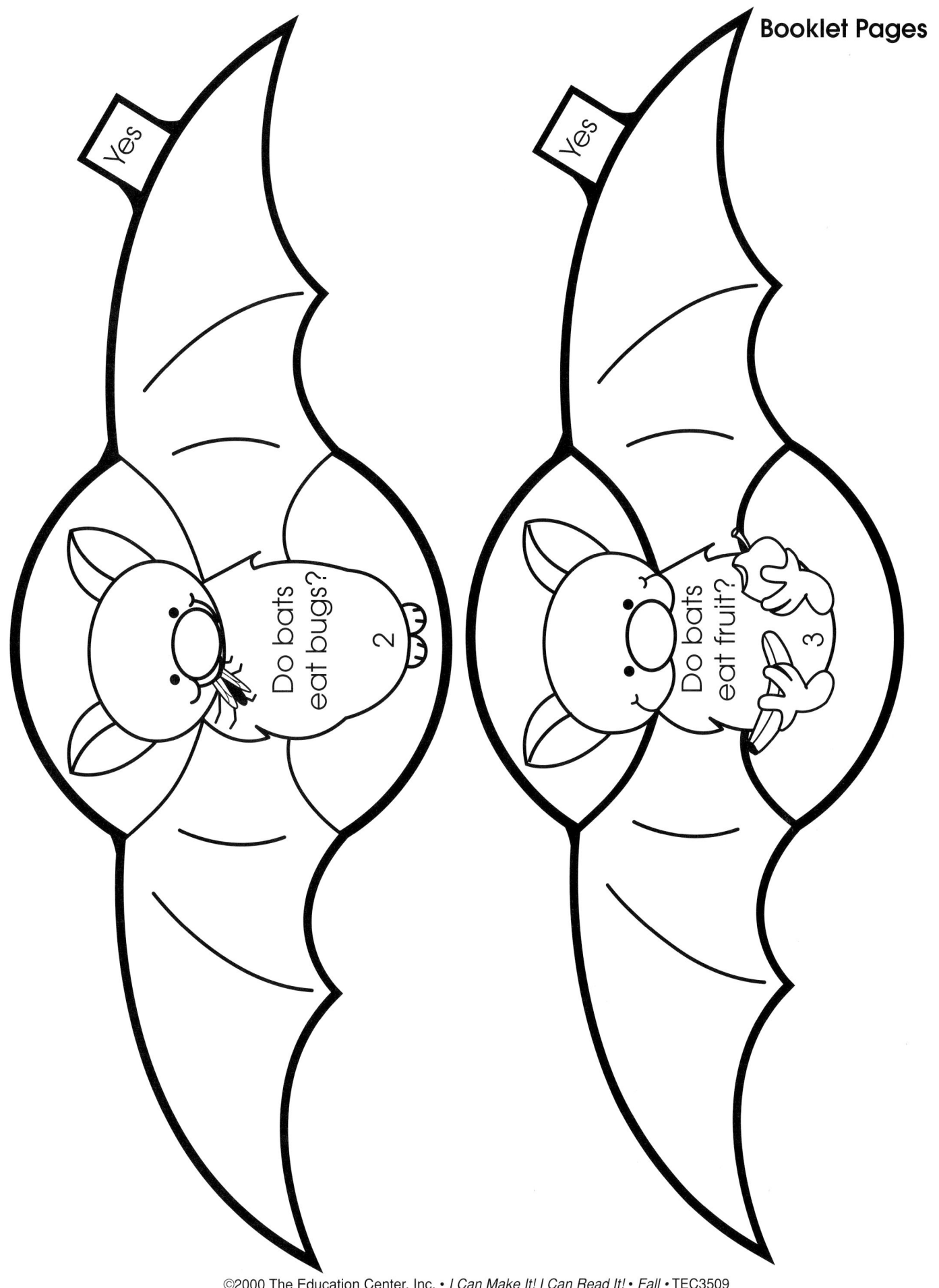

©2000 The Education Center, Inc. • *I Can Make It! I Can Read It!* • *Fall* • TEC3509

Note to the teacher: Use with "Let's Go Batty!" on page 59.

Booklet Pages

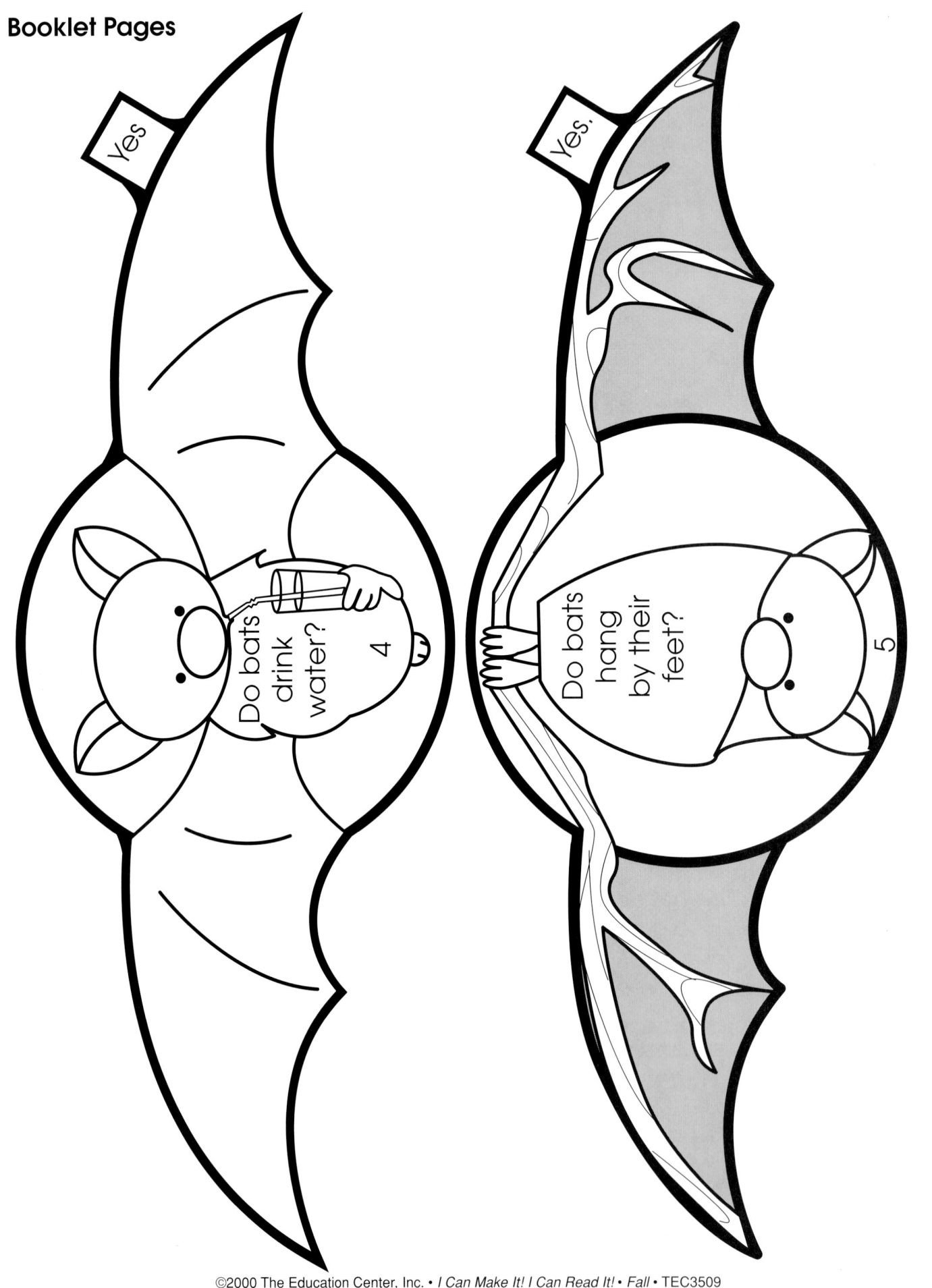

Note to the teacher: Use with "Let's Go Batty!" on page 59.

Booklet Pages

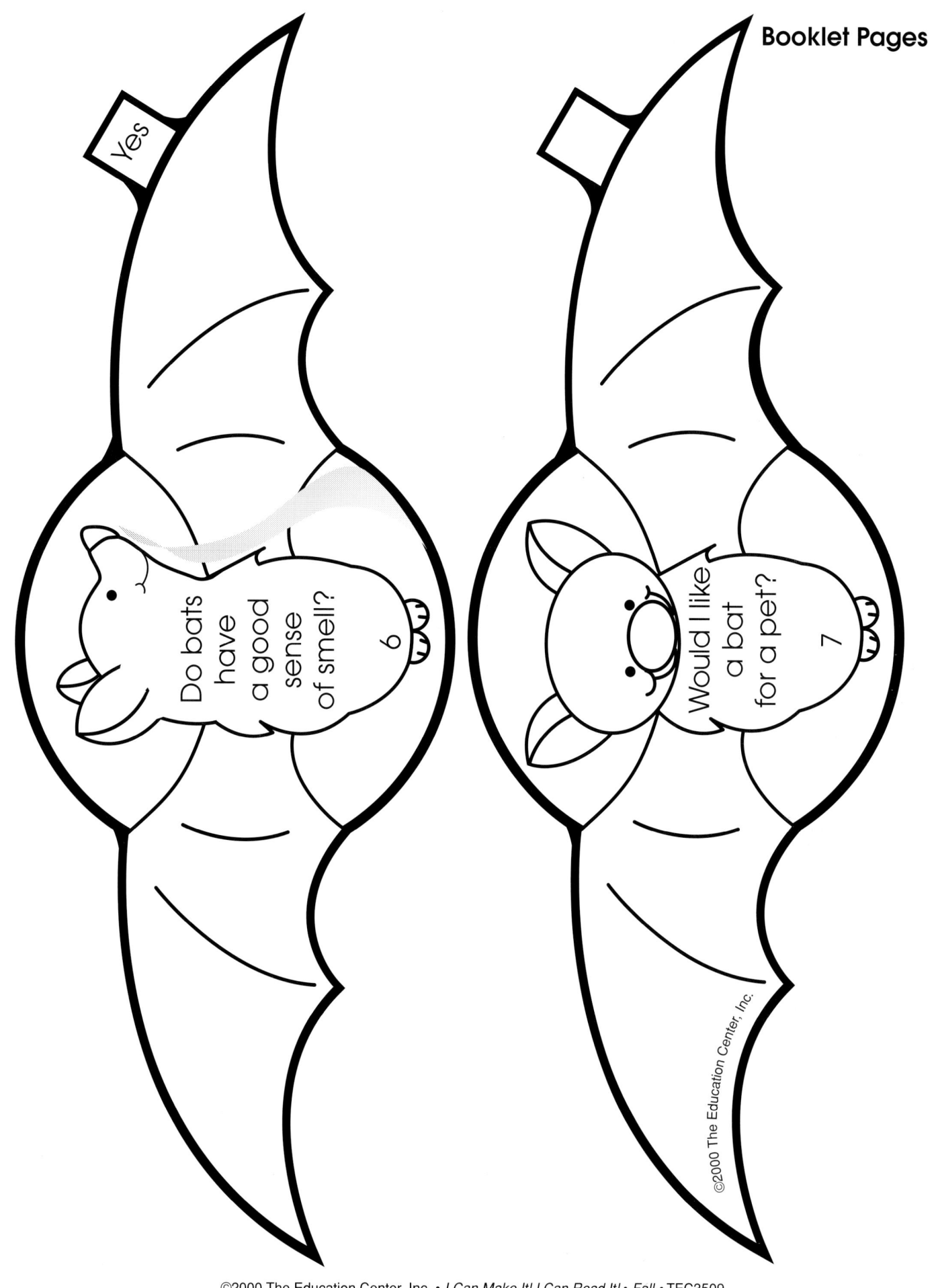

©2000 The Education Center, Inc. • *I Can Make It! I Can Read It!* • Fall • TEC3509

Note to the teacher: Use with "Let's Go Batty!" on page 59.

THE BUSY SPIDER

Spin a web of excitement into your reading program with this spider booklet! Give each student a copy of pages 65–69 and an 18" length of yarn. Have students color the pages. Then instruct each student to cut out the patterns and booklet pages on the bold outer lines. Remind students not to cut on the thin black lines. Next, demonstrate how to fold the booklet pages in half so that the illustrations show. Instruct each student to lightly glue the inside edges of each folded page. To make the doors on booklet pages 3 and 4 open and close, have the student cut on the bold line of the door on page 3. (As she cuts the door on page 3, she will be cutting the door on page 4.) Then instruct her to glue the doors together. Next, direct her to assemble her pages in order. Staple the pages together at the left-hand side of the booklet. Have her glue the cover web on the cover where indicated. Then instruct her to glue one end of the yarn to the back of the spider and the other end to the cover web. Allow the glue to dry for 30 minutes. Read with students a completed booklet, moving the spider along the dotted line of each page. Then invite each student to practice reading her booklet with a friend, tucking her spider into the web when she is finished. Send the booklet home so that family members can be caught in a web of reading!

CREATIVE DECORATING OPTIONS

- Use black yarn to outline the cover web.
- Use silver puffy paint to outline the cover web.

Read aloud to students Margaret Bloy Graham's *Be Nice to Spiders* (Harper & Row, Publishers; 1967). Then encourage students to research and list interesting facts about spiders.

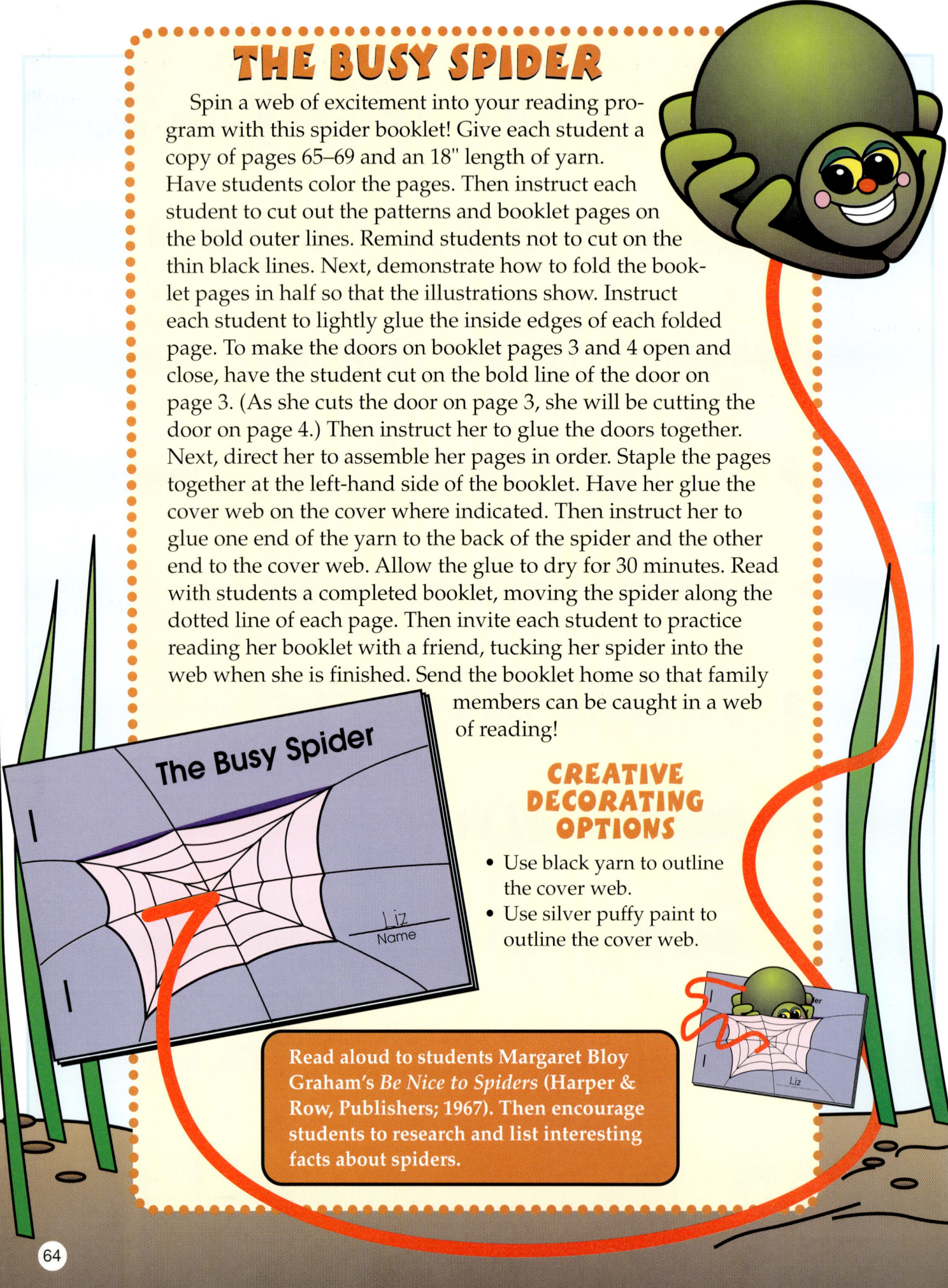

Booklet Patterns and Cover

Spider

Cover Web

Cover

The Busy Spider

Put glue on the shaded area.

Name

©2000 The Education Center, Inc.

©2000 The Education Center, Inc. • *I Can Make It! I Can Read It!* • Fall • TEC3509

Note to the teacher: Use with "The Busy Spider" on page 64.

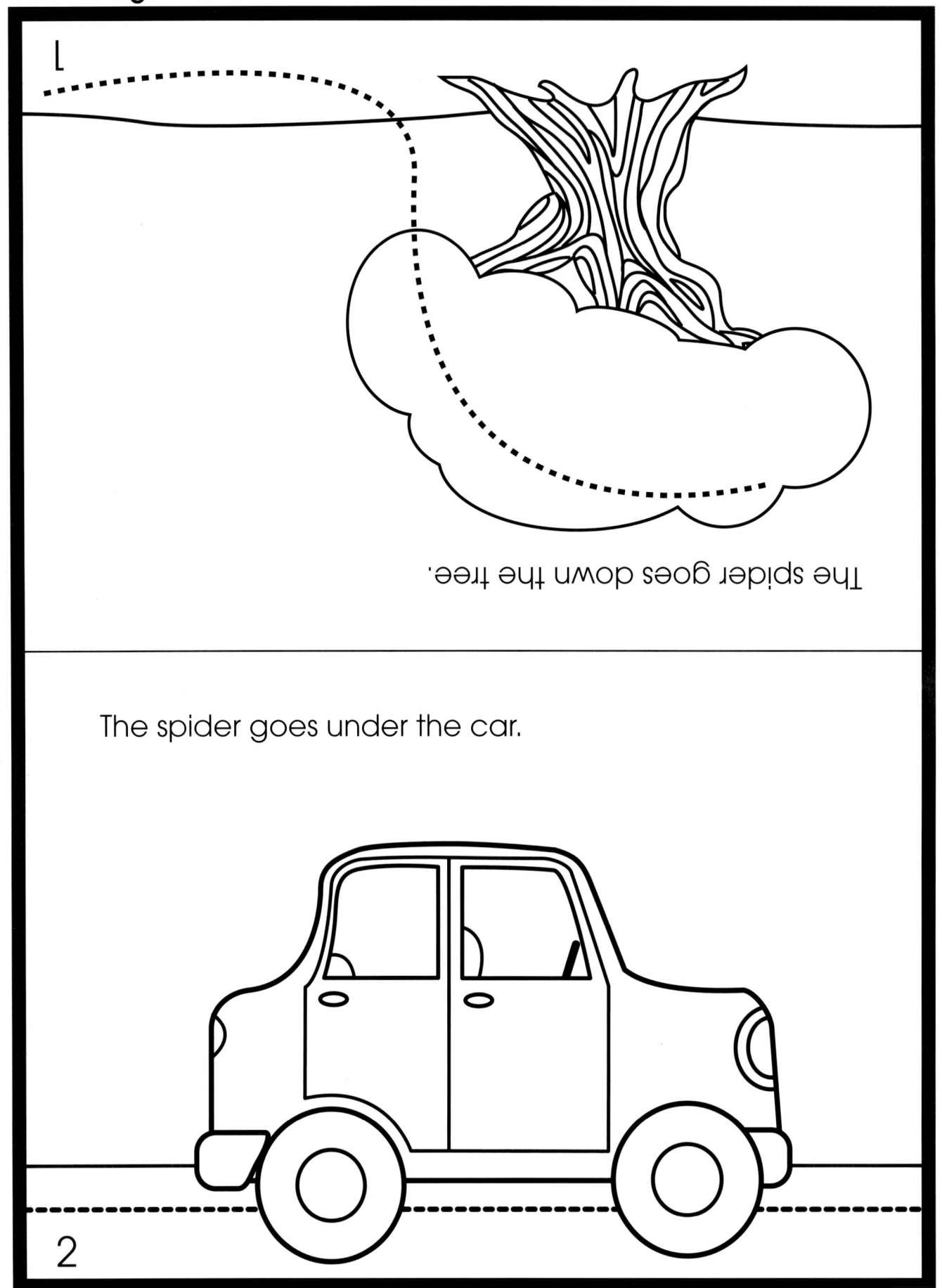

The spider goes down the tree.

The spider goes under the car.

Booklet Pages

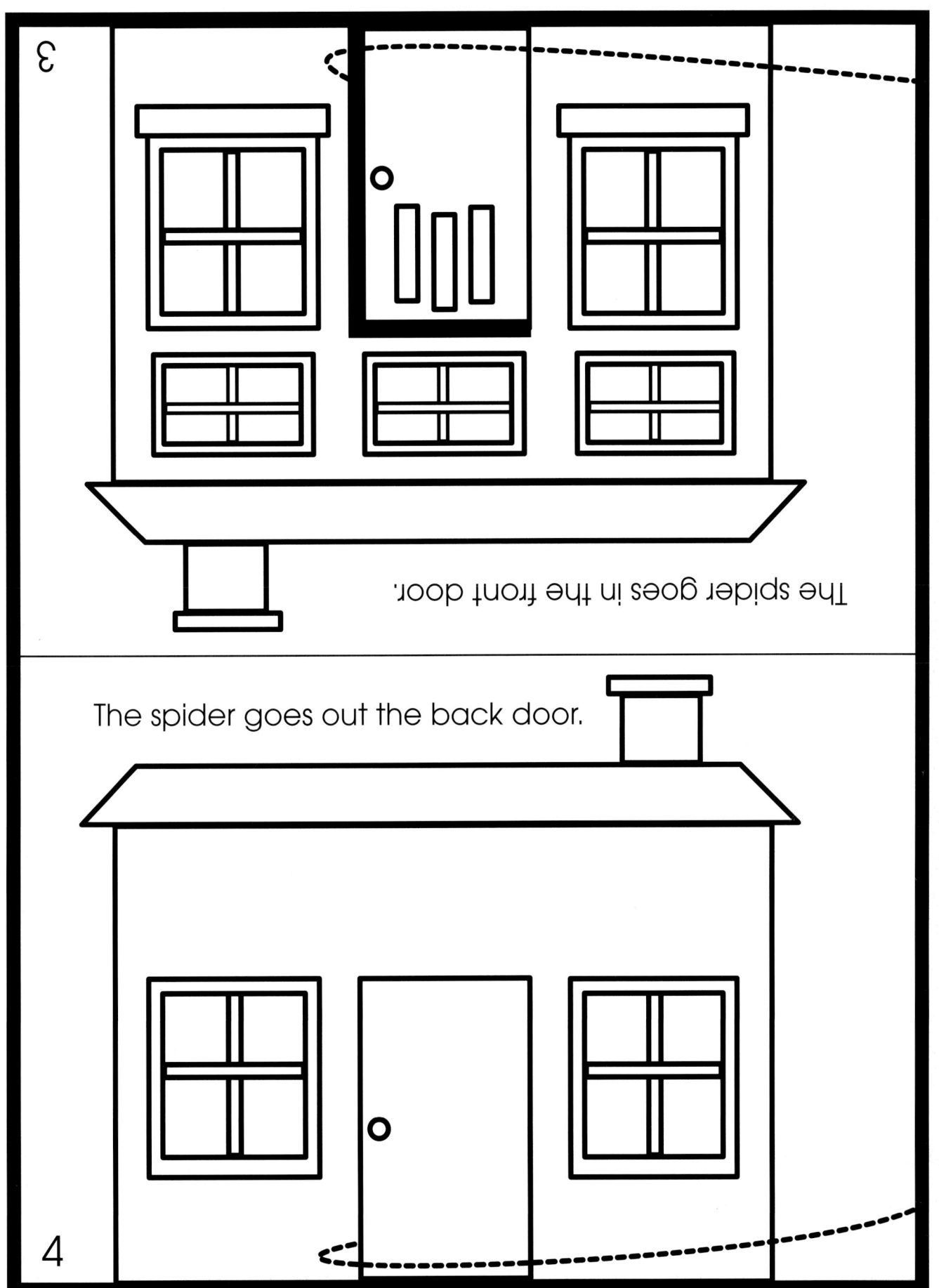

3

The spider goes in the front door.

The spider goes out the back door.

4

©2000 The Education Center, Inc. • *I Can Make It! I Can Read It! • Fall* • TEC3509

Note to the teacher: Use with "The Busy Spider" on page 64.

Booklet Pages

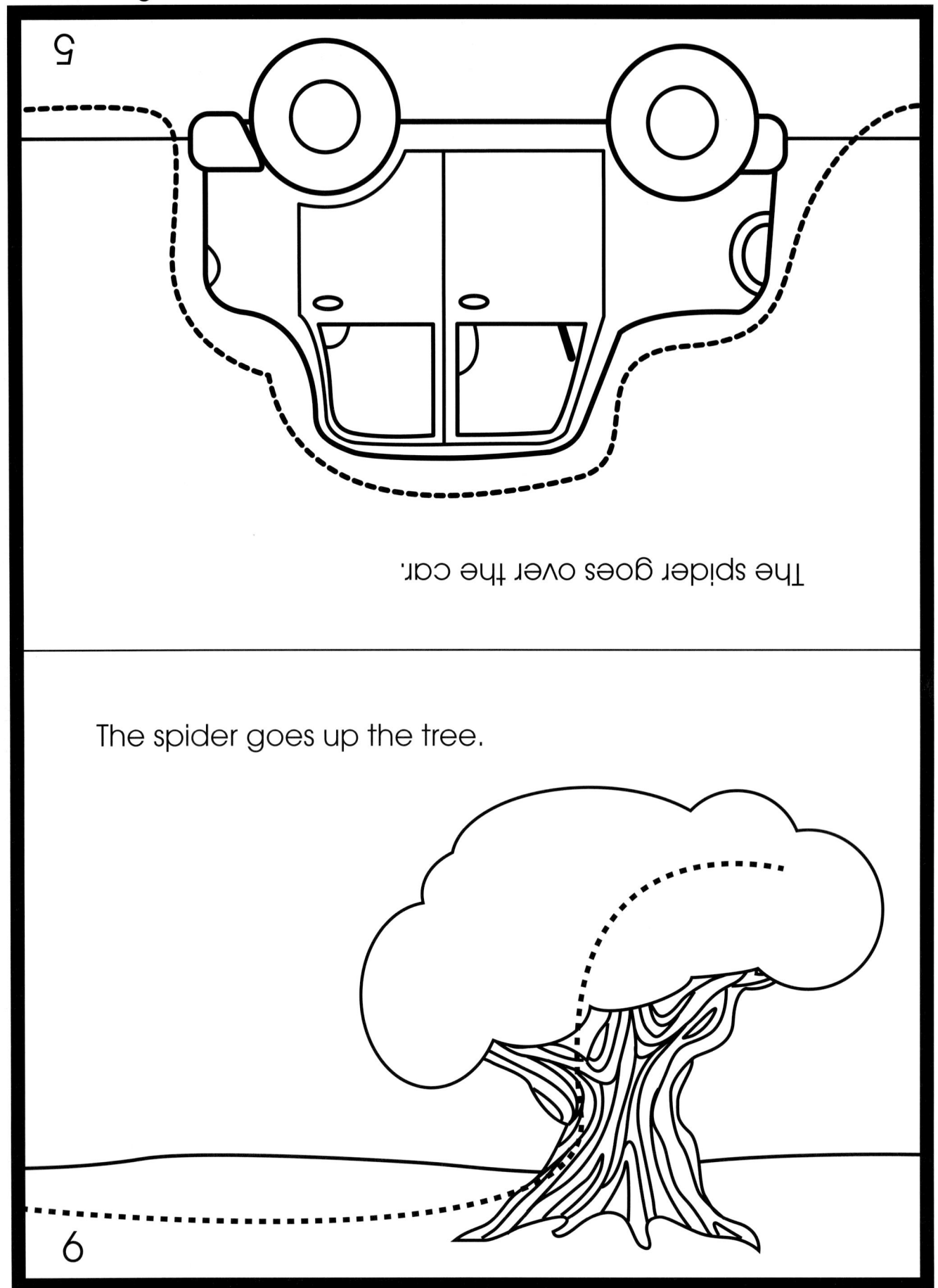

The spider goes over the car.

The spider goes up the tree.

HELLO, MR. SCARECROW!

Young readers will find there's nothing scary about reading with this fun-filled interactive booklet! Give each student a copy of pages 71–74. Instruct students to color the scarecrow patterns, cover, animal cards, and illustrated booklet pages. Then have each student cut out the patterns, cover, cards, and booklet pages on the bold lines. Next, direct the student to glue Mr. Scarecrow's top and bottom together as indicated. Then have him carefully glue the pocket to Mr. Scarecrow where indicated. Allow the glue to dry for 30 minutes. Next, instruct the student to stack his pages in order, starting with the cover. Then have him staple the booklet pages to the left-hand side of Mr. Scarecrow's pant leg. Once all the booklets are assembled, read the story with students. Have each student place the animal cards beside his booklet. As each animal is read about, the student places the matching animal card in Mr. Scarecrow's pocket. Provide time for students to practice reading with a friend before sending the booklets home for family members to enjoy. Mr. Scarecrow will let your young readers hang around his garden as long as they want!

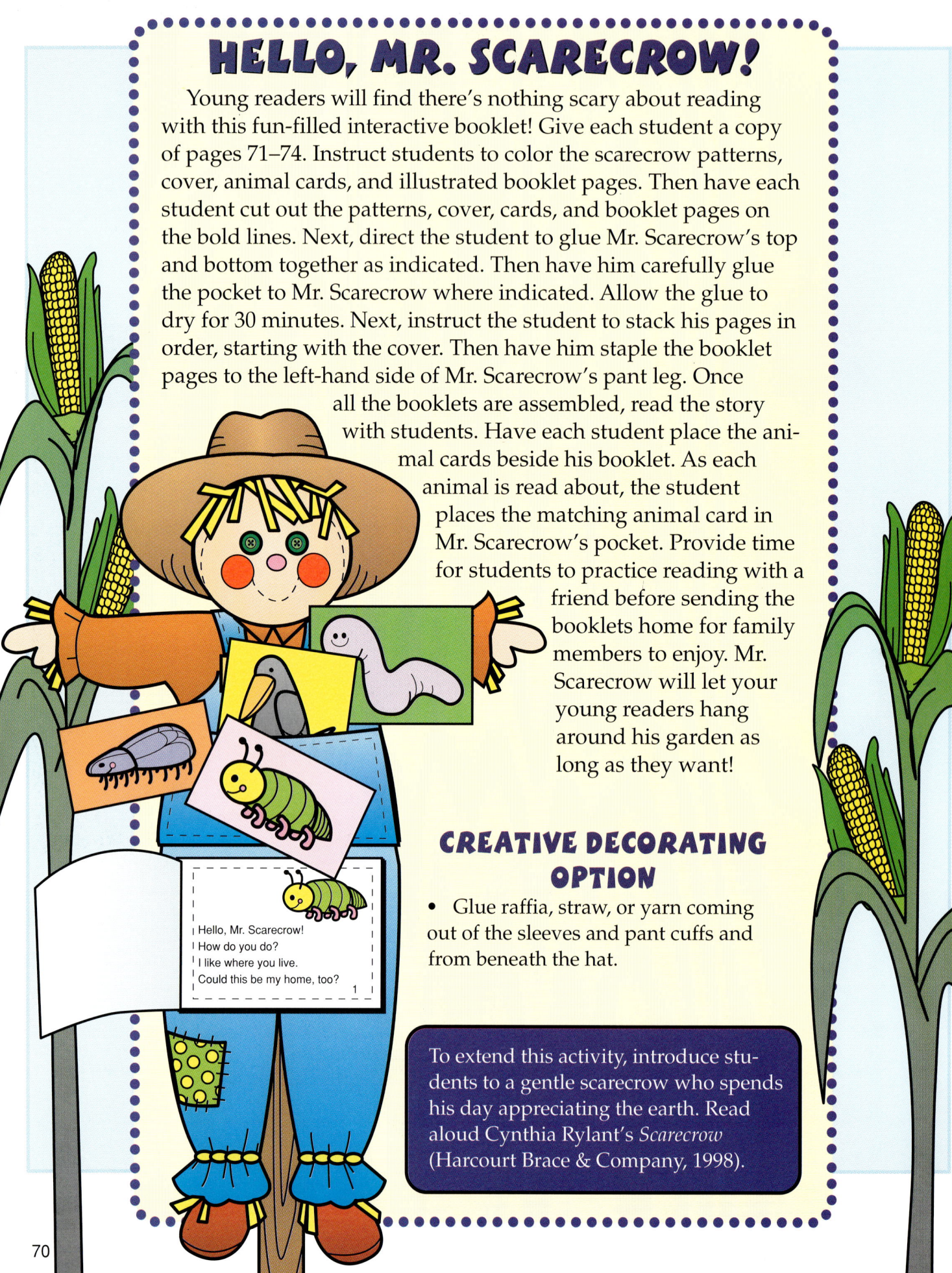

CREATIVE DECORATING OPTION

- Glue raffia, straw, or yarn coming out of the sleeves and pant cuffs and from beneath the hat.

To extend this activity, introduce students to a gentle scarecrow who spends his day appreciating the earth. Read aloud Cynthia Rylant's *Scarecrow* (Harcourt Brace & Company, 1998).

Booklet Pattern

Mr. Scarecrow Top

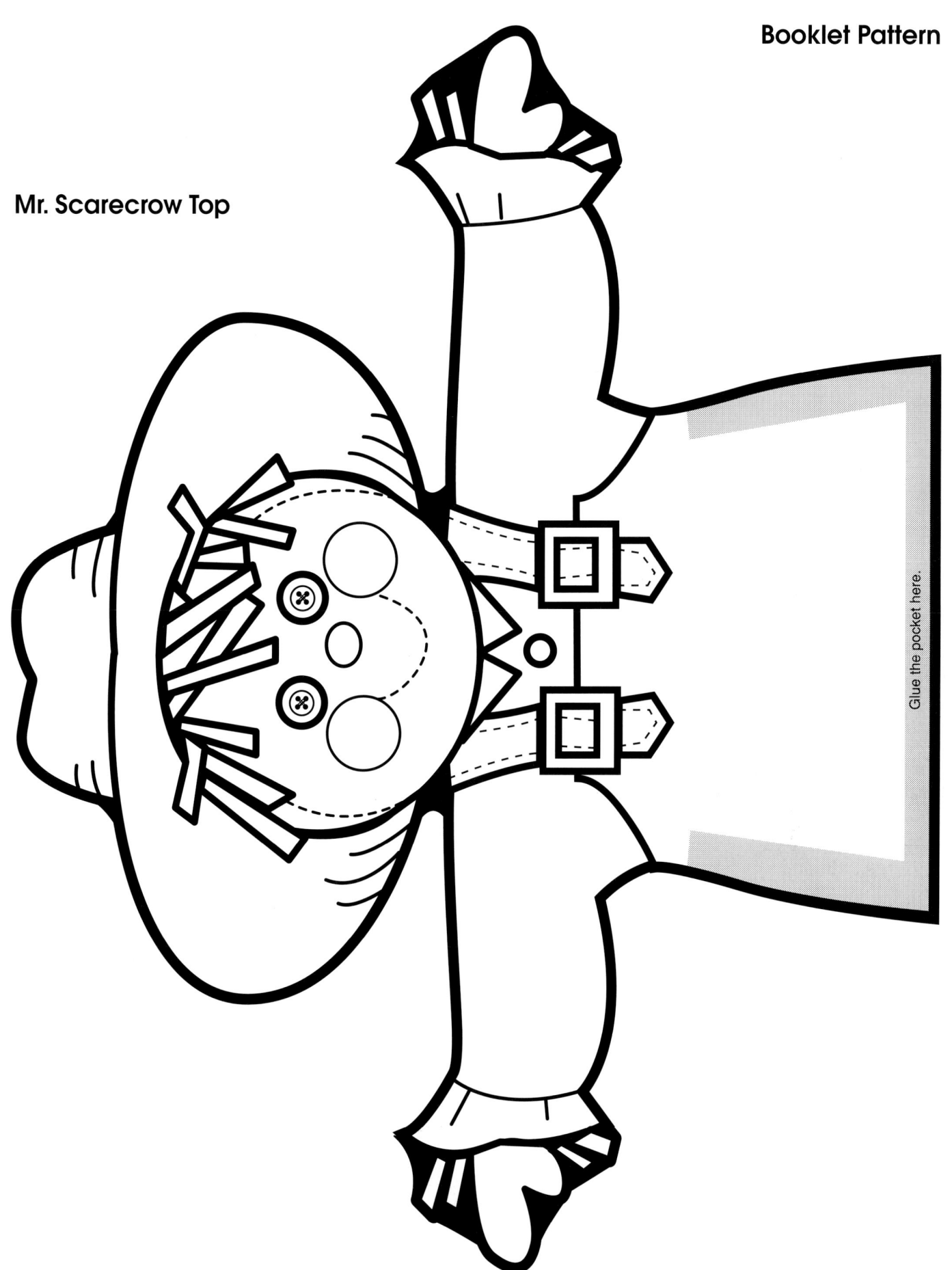

Glue the pocket here.

©2000 The Education Center, Inc. • *I Can Make It! I Can Read It!* • Fall • TEC3509

Note to the teacher: Use with "Hello, Mr. Scarecrow!" on page 70.

Booklet Patterns

Mr. Scarecrow Bottom

Pocket

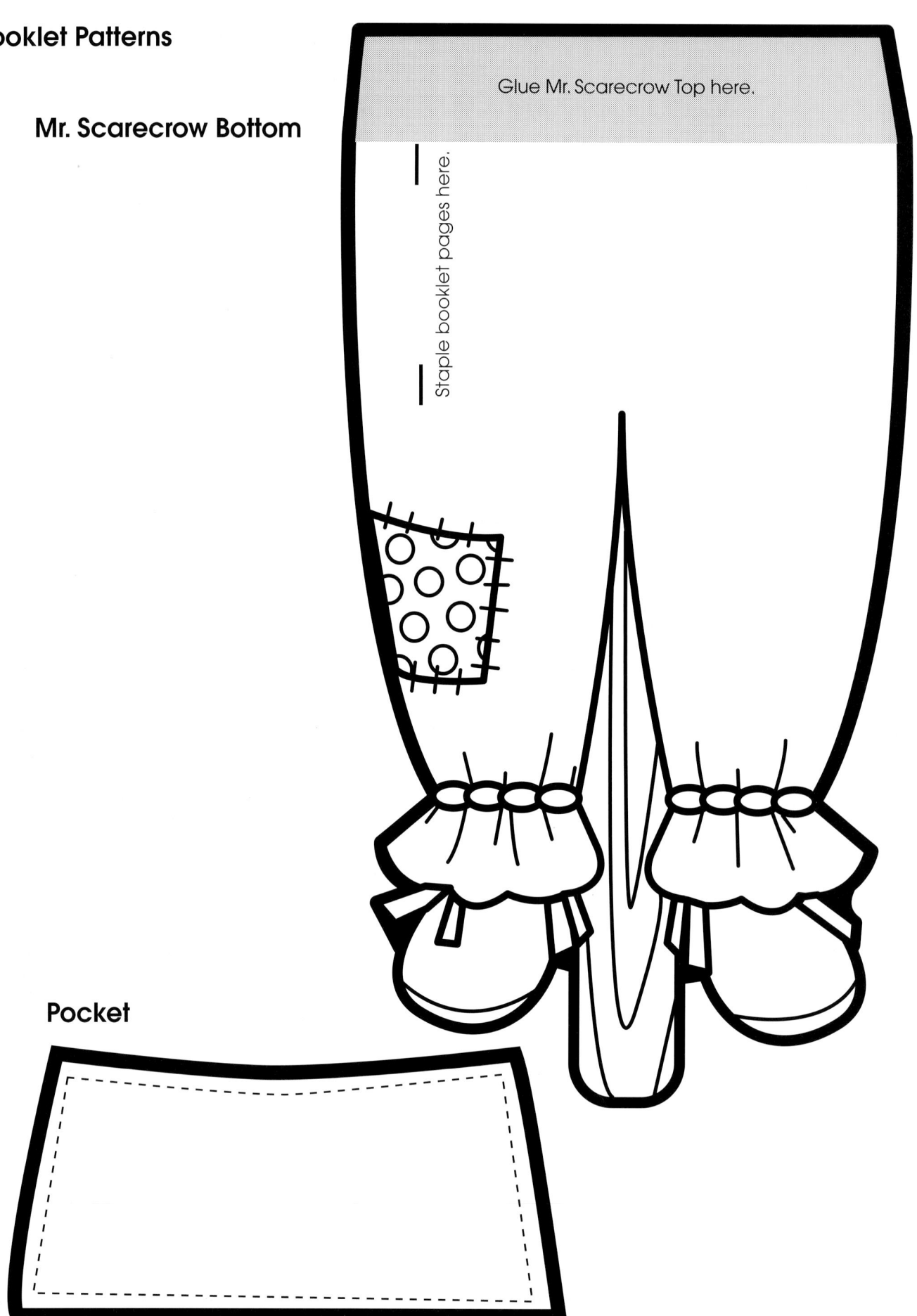

©2000 The Education Center, Inc. • *I Can Make It! I Can Read It!* • *Fall* • TEC3509

Note to the teacher: Use with "Hello, Mr. Scarecrow!" on page 70.

Booklet Cover, Pages and Cards
Animal Cards
Mrs. Beetle

Mrs. Bug

Cover

Hello, Mr. Scarecrow!

_____
Name

©2000 The Education Center, Inc.

Mr. Crow

Booklet Pages

Hello, Mr. Scarecrow!
How do you do?
I like where you live.
Could this be my home, too?

1

No, Mrs. Bug,
There is not a spot
In my fine garden.
I think NOT!

2

Mr. Worm

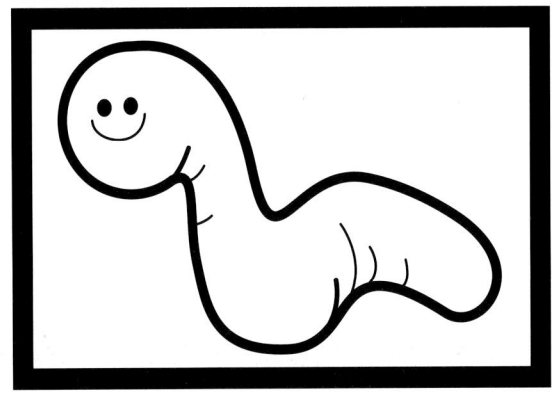

©2000 The Education Center, Inc. • *I Can Make It! I Can Read It!* • Fall • TEC3509

Note to the teacher: Use with "Hello, Mr. Scarecrow!" on page 70.

Booklet Pages

ONE DARK NIGHT

Boost reader confidence with this pick from the pumpkin patch—a "spook-tacular" story that's repetitive and predictable! Give each student a copy of pages 76–79. Read the booklet pages with students. Then instruct each student to color his booklet pages to match the color words in the text. (Remind students to color lightly over the text so the story can be read.) Next have him cut out the booklet pages on the bold outer lines. Then direct him to link the pages by gluing together the pumpkins where indicated. Once the glue is dry, demonstrate how to accordion-fold the booklet along the thin lines of each pumpkin. Encourage each student to practice reading his booklet with a partner before taking it home to read to family members.

CREATIVE DECORATING OPTION

- Glue green construction paper leaves to the top of each pumpkin.

Extend this booklet-making activity by reading aloud Steven Kroll's *The Biggest Pumpkin Ever* (Cartwheel Books, 1993). Use this book as a springboard to discuss with students how pumpkins grow.

Booklet Pages

Note to the teacher: Use with "One Dark Night" on page 75.

Booklet Pages

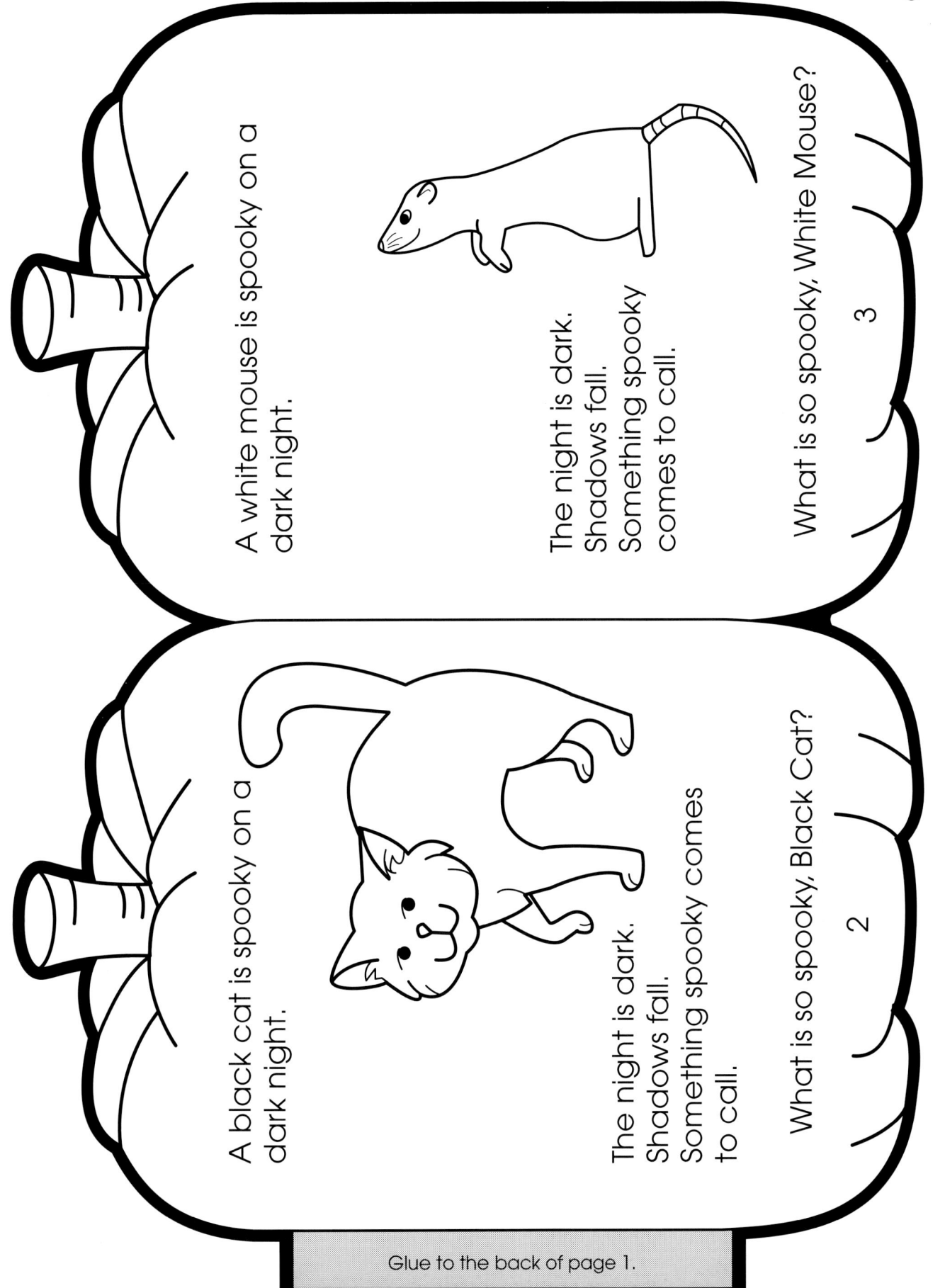

A white mouse is spooky on a dark night.

The night is dark.
Shadows fall.
Something spooky comes to call.

What is so spooky, White Mouse?

3

A black cat is spooky on a dark night.

The night is dark.
Shadows fall.
Something spooky comes to call.

What is so spooky, Black Cat?

2

Glue to the back of page 1.

Note to the teacher: Use with "One Dark Night" on page 75.

Booklet Pages

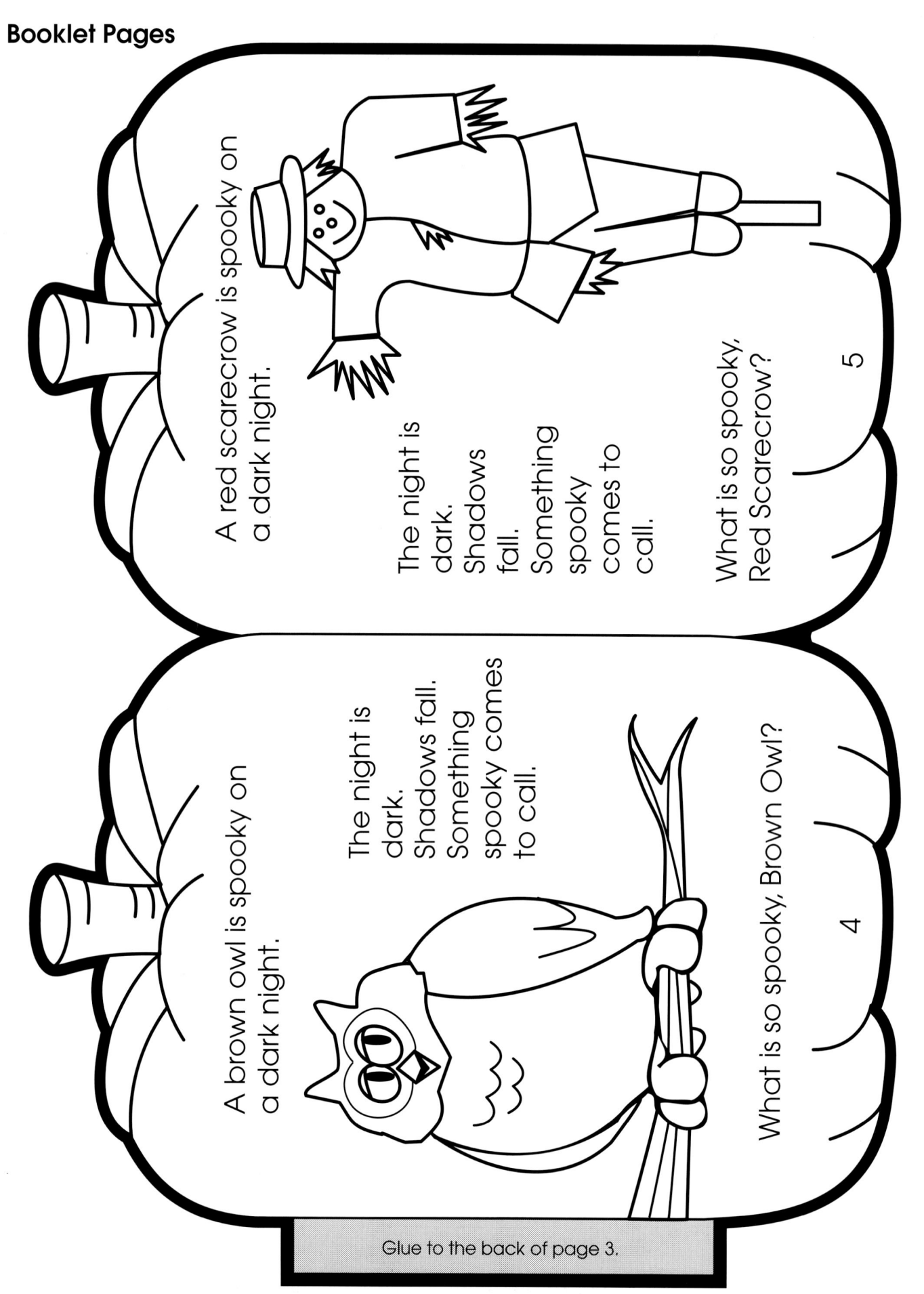

A red scarecrow is spooky on a dark night.

The night is dark.
Shadows fall.
Something spooky comes to call.

What is so spooky, Red Scarecrow?

5

A brown owl is spooky on a dark night.

The night is dark.
Shadows fall.
Something spooky comes to call.

What is so spooky, Brown Owl?

4

Glue to the back of page 3.

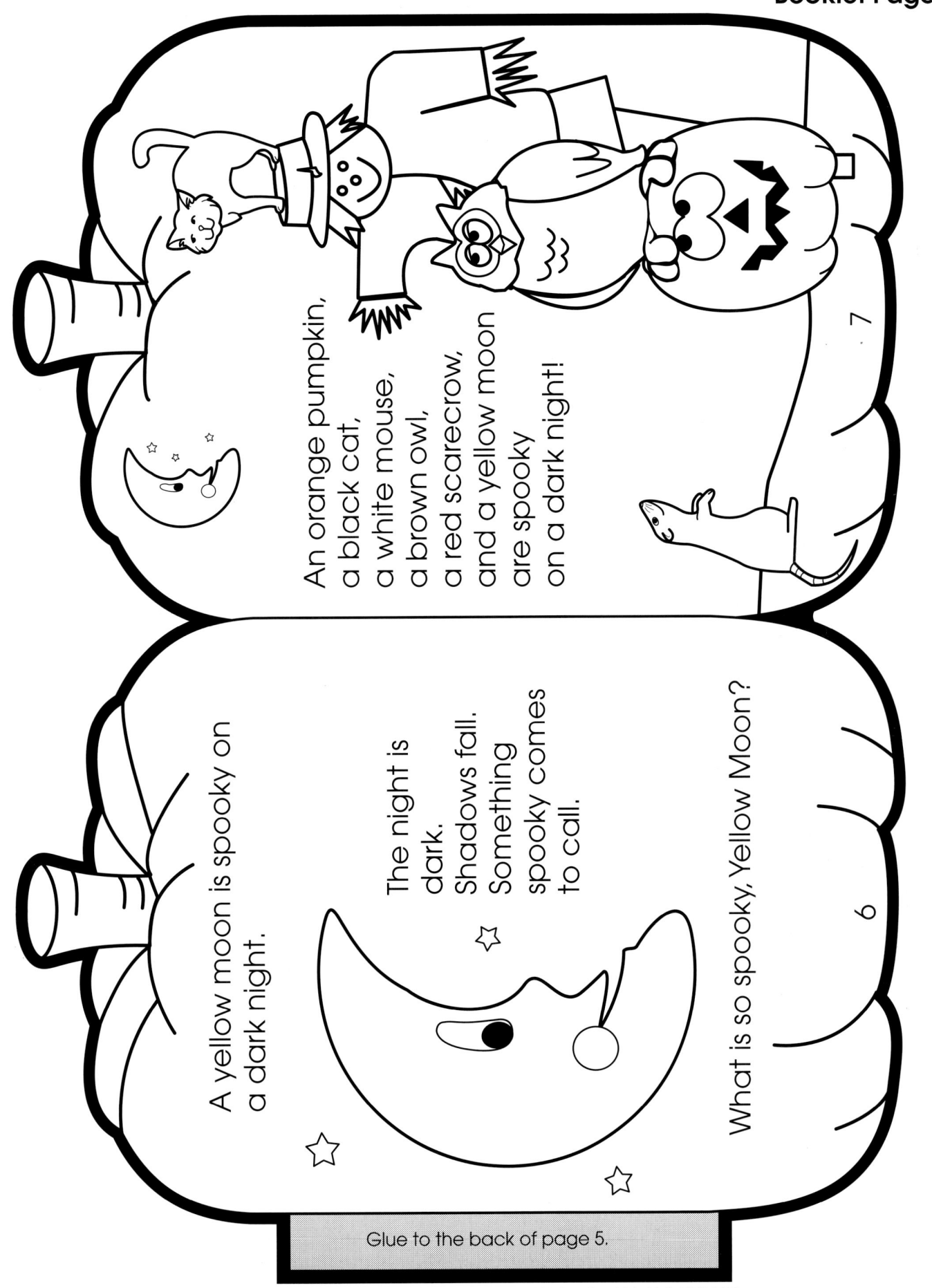

NATIVE AMERICAN ROCK ART

Reading is really rocking with this interactive Native American booklet! Give each student a copy of pages 81–85. Explain to students that some Native Americans once used picture symbols similar to those on page 81 to write messages on rocks. Read the pages with students, encouraging them to guess the meaning of each symbol on booklet page 1. *(Answers: wolf, dog, or coyote; mountain sheep; and rabbit)* Then have each student color and cut out her picture cards, cover, and booklet pages. For each booklet page with boxes, instruct her to glue the appropriate picture cards to match the text. When the glue has dried, invite the student to add her own illustrations to the booklet pages. Then direct the student to stack her completed pages in numerical order, placing the cover on top. Have her align the pages with the rock on booklet page 7 and staple the booklet on the left-hand side. Provide time for students to practice reading their booklets with friends. Then encourage them to take their booklets home to share with family members. Reading can be easy as 🥧!

CREATIVE DECORATING OPTIONS

- Using fine markers, decorate the cover with the student's inventive picture writing.
- Outline the cover with glue. Sprinkle sand on the glue.

To extend this activity, have each youngster paint a rock with symbols she has created. Then provide time for each student to share her rock's message with the class.

Picture Cards

Picture Cards and Cover

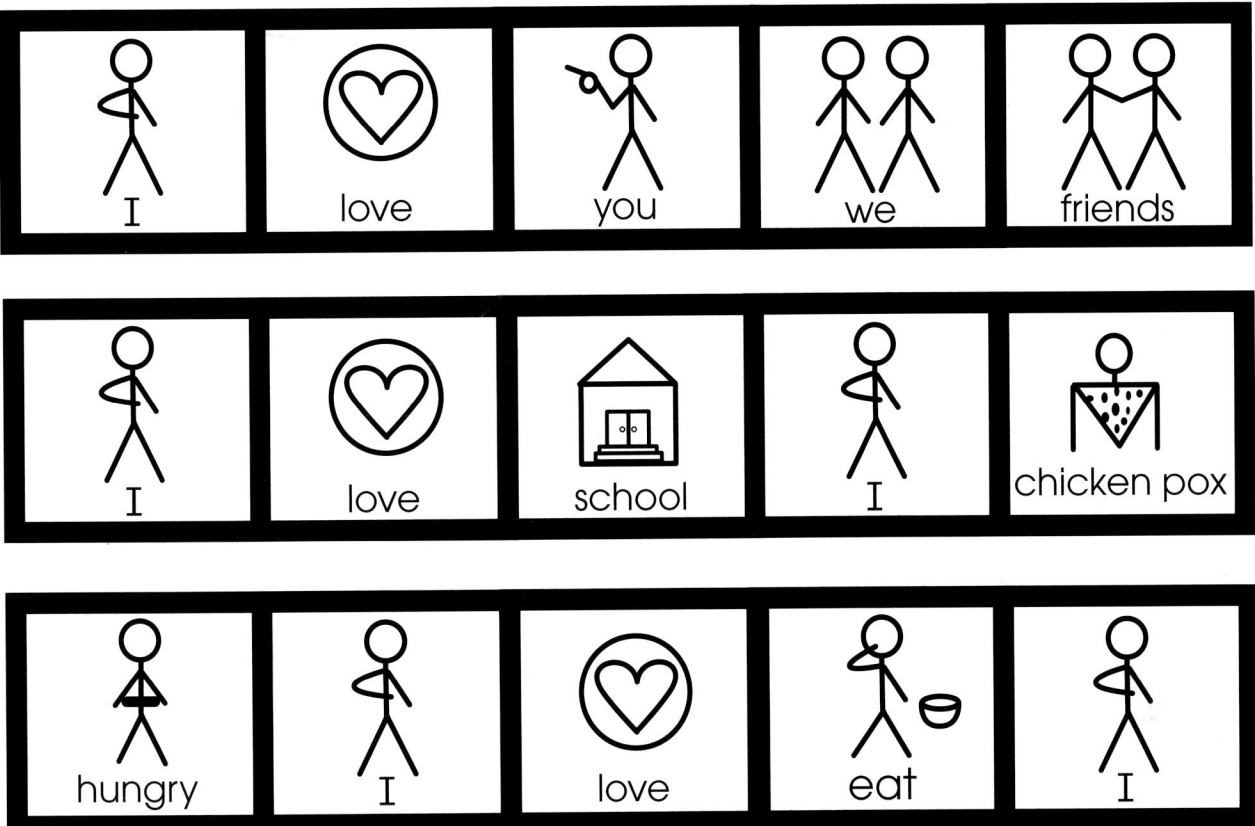

Cover

Note to the teacher: Use with "Native American Rock Art" on page 80.

Booklet Pages

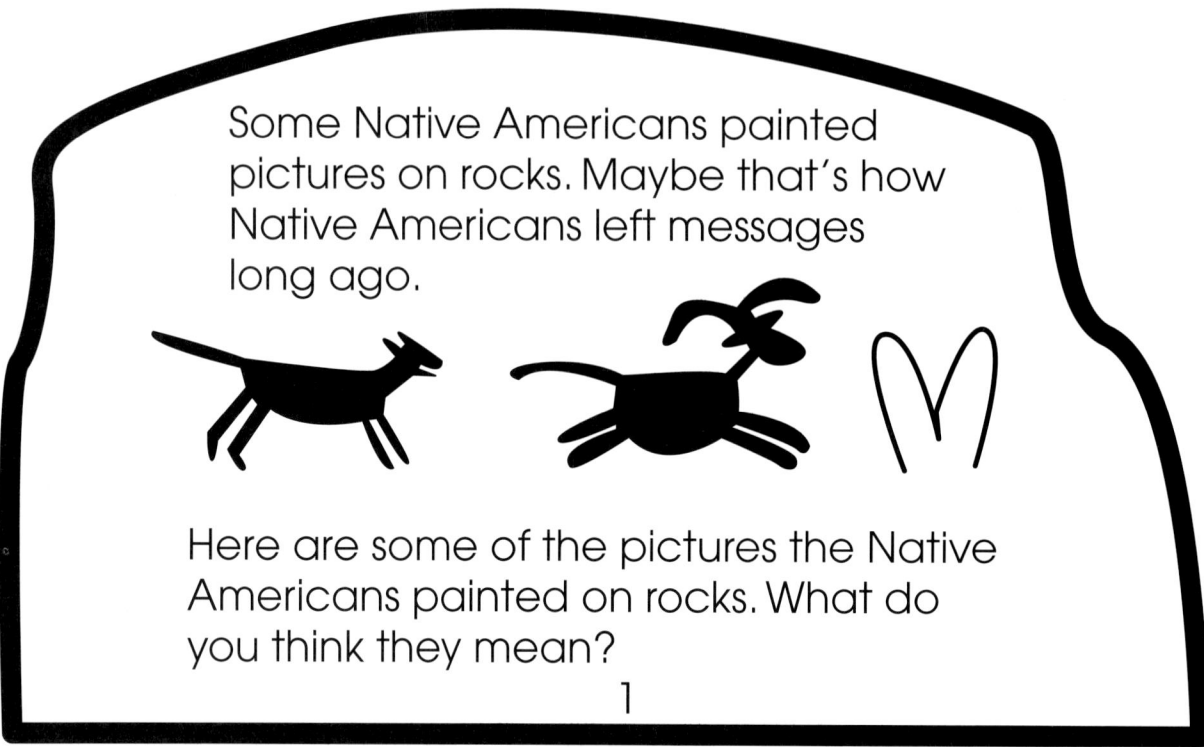

Some Native Americans painted pictures on rocks. Maybe that's how Native Americans left messages long ago.

Here are some of the pictures the Native Americans painted on rocks. What do you think they mean?

1

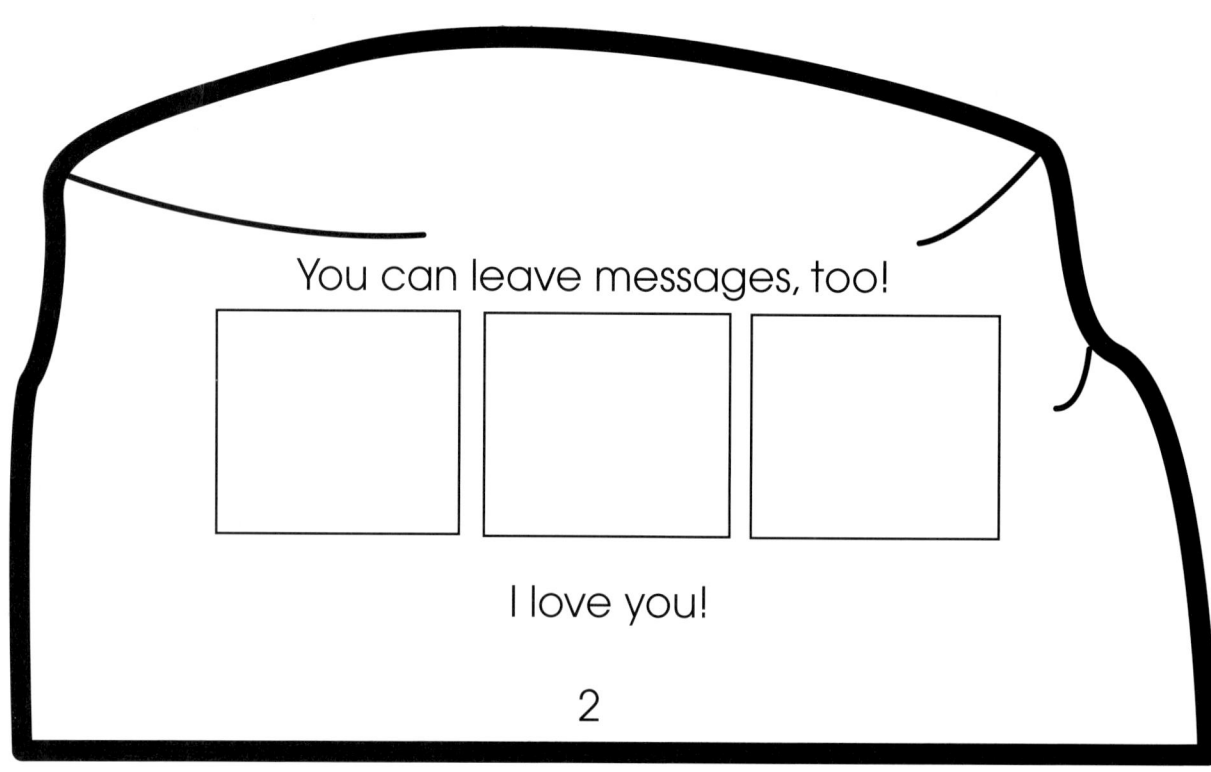

You can leave messages, too!

I love you!

2

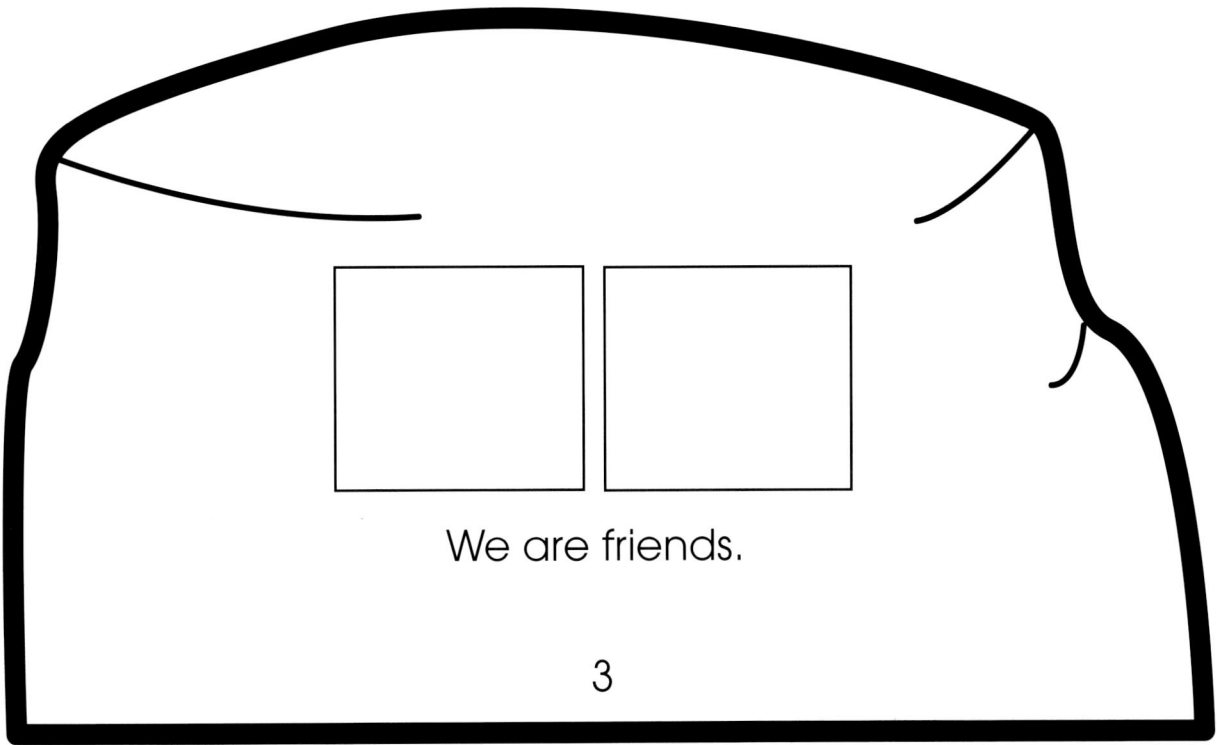

We are friends.

3

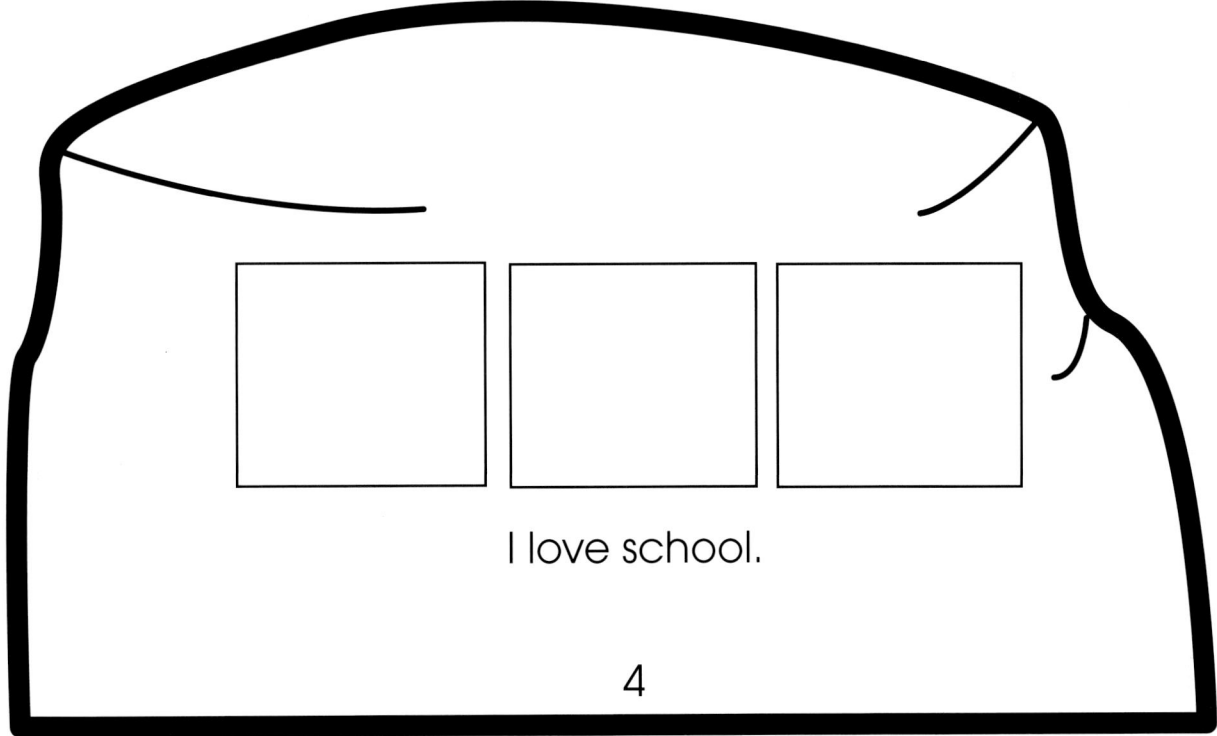

I love school.

4

Booklet Pages

I have the chicken pox.

5

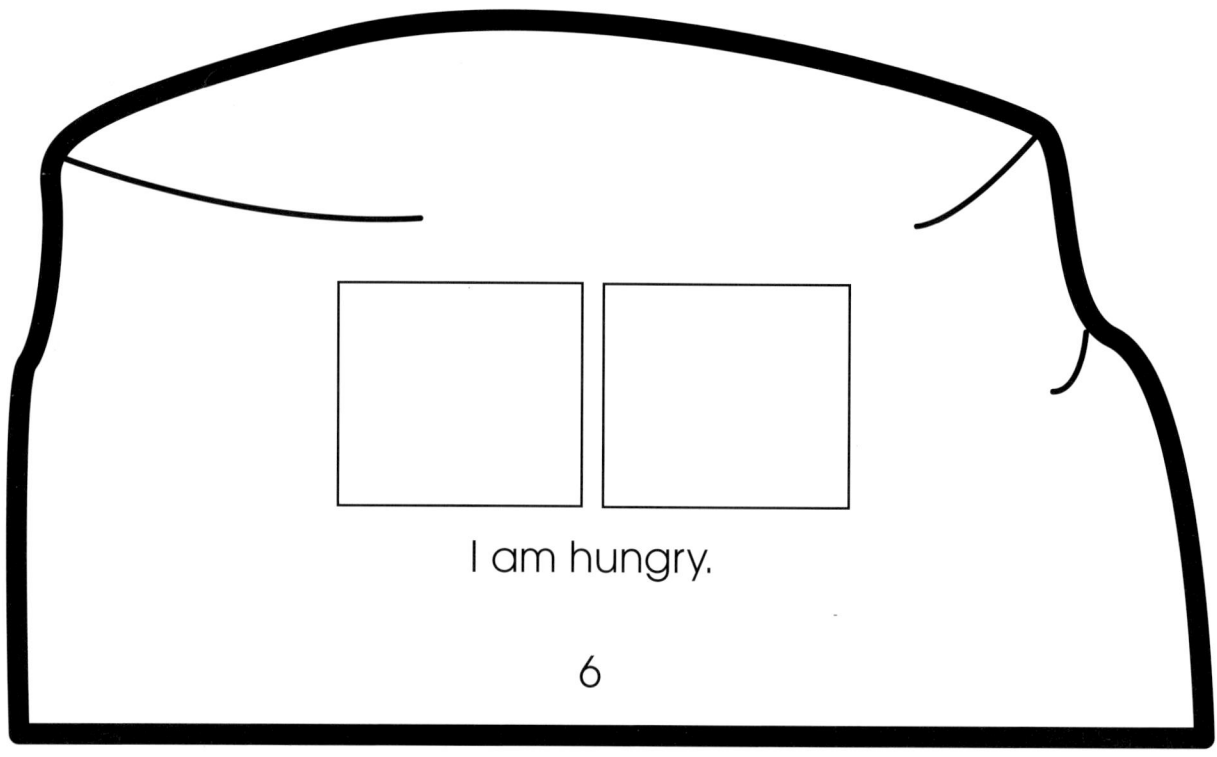

I am hungry.

6

Booklet Pages

I love to eat.

7

©2000 The Education Center, Inc. • *I Can Make It! I Can Read It!* • Fall • TEC3509

Note to the teacher: Use with "Native American Rock Art" on page 80.

PILGRIM CHILDREN

Young readers will discover how different life was for Pilgrim children with this informative booklet. Give each student a copy of page 87. To make the booklet, each student personalizes it, colors it, and follows the directions provided below. Once students have completed their booklets, have them practice reading in pairs. Then invite students to take their booklets home to share with family members.

Directions for folding the Pilgrim booklet:
1. Cut out the booklet page on the bold lines.
2. Fold the paper in half lengthwise, pictures facing out.
3. Leaving the paper folded, fold it in half widthwise and then in half widthwise again.
4. Unfold the paper to reveal eight rectangles.
5. Fold the paper in half widthwise, pictures facing out.
6. Cut on the thin center line.
7. Unfold the paper. Fold it in half lengthwise, pictures facing out.
8. Hold the two ends and push together as shown at the right.
9. Fold the booklet so that the cover page is on top.

CREATIVE DECORATING OPTION

- Before making class copies of the booklet pages, white-out the illustrations. Have students create their own illustrations.

Extend this booklet-making activity by introducing students to a typical day in the life of Pilgrim children. Share Kate Waters' informative and entertaining books, *Sarah Morton's Day: A Day in the Life of a Pilgrim Girl* (Scholastic Inc., 1989) and *Samuel Eaton's Day: A Day in the Life of a Pilgrim Boy* (Scholastic Inc., 1993).

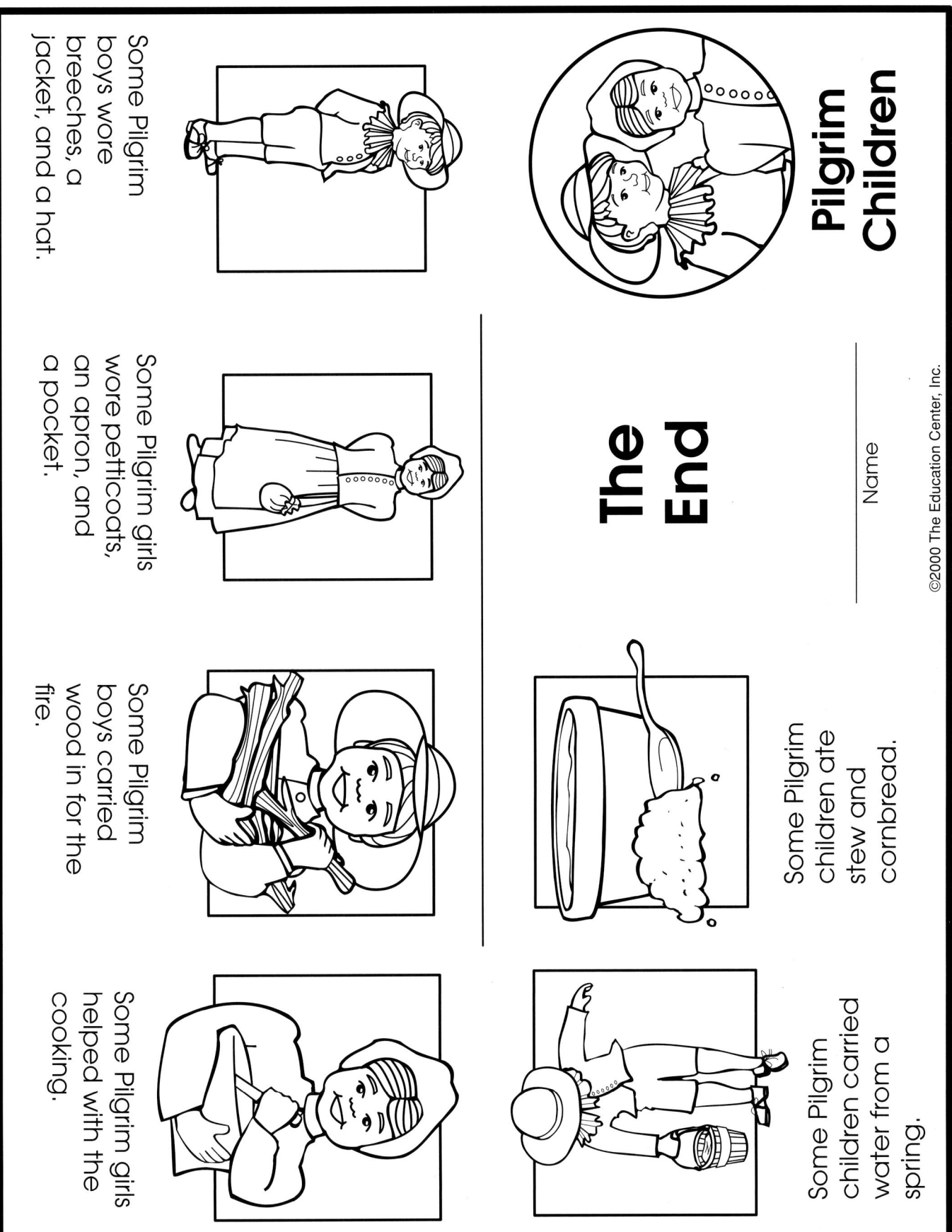

GOBBLE! GOBBLE! WHAT'S FOR LUNCH?

Young readers will have a grand time reading this interactive turkey booklet that waddles! Give each student a copy of pages 89–91 and a brad. Instruct the student to color his turkey, turkey tail, and cover. Then have him cut them out along with the booklet pages. To assemble the booklet, he stacks the booklet pages in numerical order, placing the cover on top. Then he staples the booklet to the turkey where indicated. Holding the booklet pages out of the way, help the student align the turkey and the turkey tail at the circles. Insert the brad through both patterns where indicated. Once the booklets are assembled, read the story aloud to students. As you read how the tail feathers go, encourage students to rotate their turkey tails back and forth. Next, have students take turns reading with a partner. Invite them to take their booklets home to read to family members. Parents will be tickled with these unique turkeys *and* their child's reading progress!

CREATIVE DECORATING OPTION

- Glue wiggle eyes on the turkey.
- Glue craft feathers to the turkey's tail.

To extend this activity, show students how Miguel's pet turkey is saved from being Thanksgiving dinner by reading aloud Joy Cowley's *Gracias, The Thanksgiving Turkey* (Scholastic Press, 1996).

Turkey **Booklet Pattern**

Staple cover and pages here.

Insert brad here.

©2000 The Education Center, Inc. • *I Can Make It! I Can Read It!* • Fall • TEC3509

Note to the teacher: Use with "Gobble! Gobble! What's for Lunch?" on page 88.

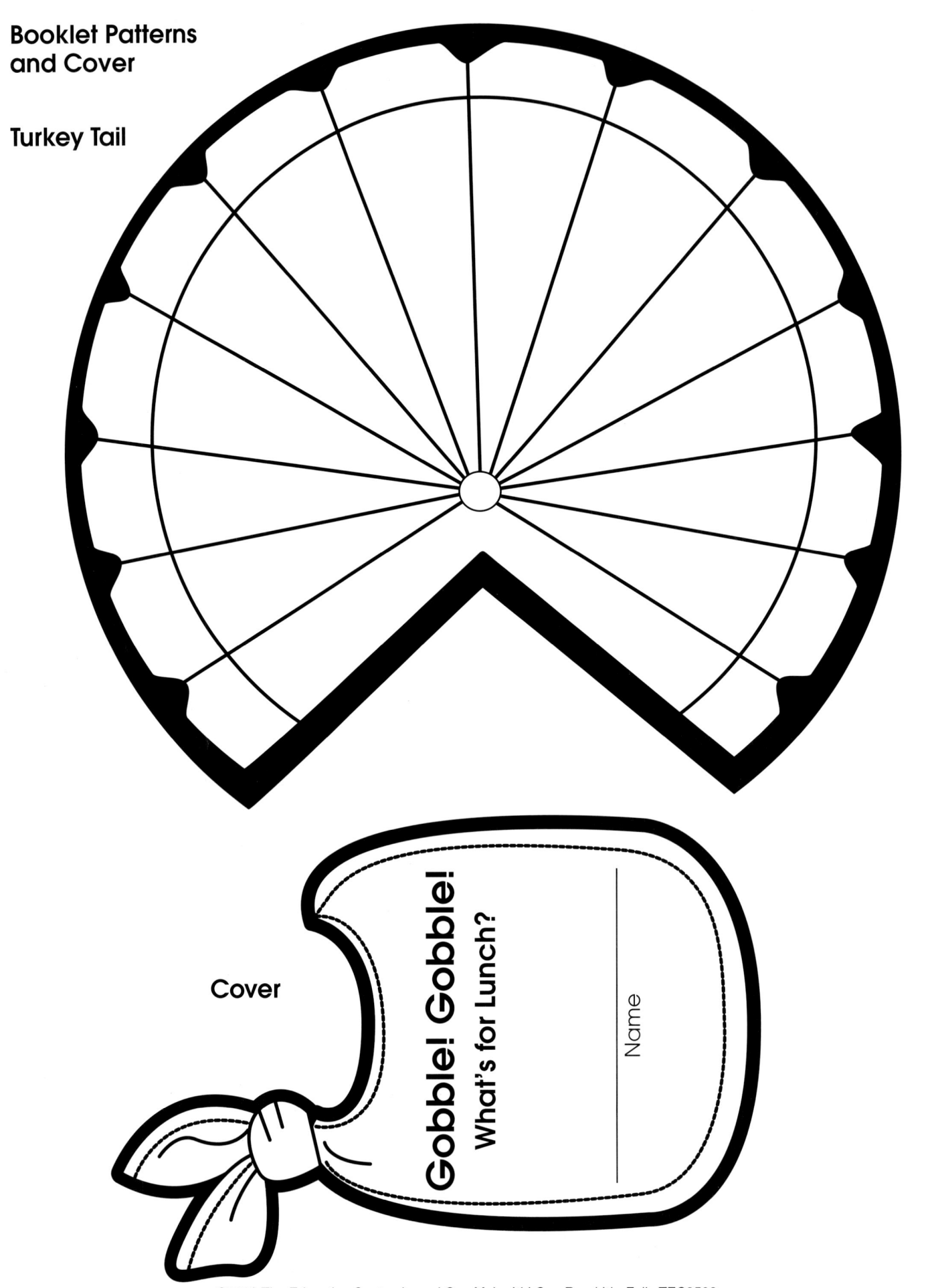

Booklet Pages

Is it marshmallows, soft and gooey?

Just the thought makes my tail feathers go *splooey, splooey!*

3

Gobble! Gobble! What will we eat?

Promise me *anything* But turkey meat!

6

Is it french fries and soda pop?

Just the thought makes my tail feathers go *flip-flop!*

2

Is it a piece of pumpkin pie?

Just the thought makes my tail feathers go *tish-shy!*

5

Is it ice cream in a dish?

Just the thought makes my tail feathers go *swish, swish!*

1

Is it hot chocolate in a mug?

Just the thought makes my tail feathers go *chug-a-lug!*

4

©2000 The Education Center, Inc. • *I Can Make It! I Can Read It!* • Fall • TEC3509

Note to the teacher: Use with "Gobble! Gobble! What's for Lunch?" on page 88.

TIME FOR HARVEST!

Students will have bushels of fun with this interactive booklet that's just right for the picking! Give each student a copy of pages 93–96. Read with students the booklet pages. Then instruct each student to color and cut out the cover, booklet pages, and patterns. (Remind students to color lightly over the text so that the story can be read.) Next, direct the student to carefully cut a slit on the dotted line of each booklet page. Have him slip the appropriate food items and the spoon into the slits and then glue them into place. Instruct him to place his booklet pages in numerical order, placing the cover on top. Staple the pages together on the left-hand side of the booklet. Provide time for each youngster to read his completed booklet with a partner before taking it home to read with family members. You'll reap a harvest of good readers!

CREATIVE DECORATING OPTIONS

- Glue colorful leaves to the base of the cover.
- Use puffy paint to outline the food items and spoon.
- Use brads insteads of staples to bind the pages on the left edge.

To extend this activity, read aloud a humorous tale of how Bear and Hare share a gardening relationship in *Tops & Bottoms* by Janet Stevens (Harcourt Brace & Company, 1995).

Booklet Cover and Page

cover

Time for Harvest!

©2000 The Education Center, Inc.

Name

It is time for harvest!
We will pick pumpkins.
We will pick beans.
We will pick apples and berries.

1

©2000 The Education Center, Inc. • *I Can Make It! I Can Read It!* • Fall • TEC3509

Note to the teacher: Use with "Time for Harvest!" on page 92.

Booklet Pages

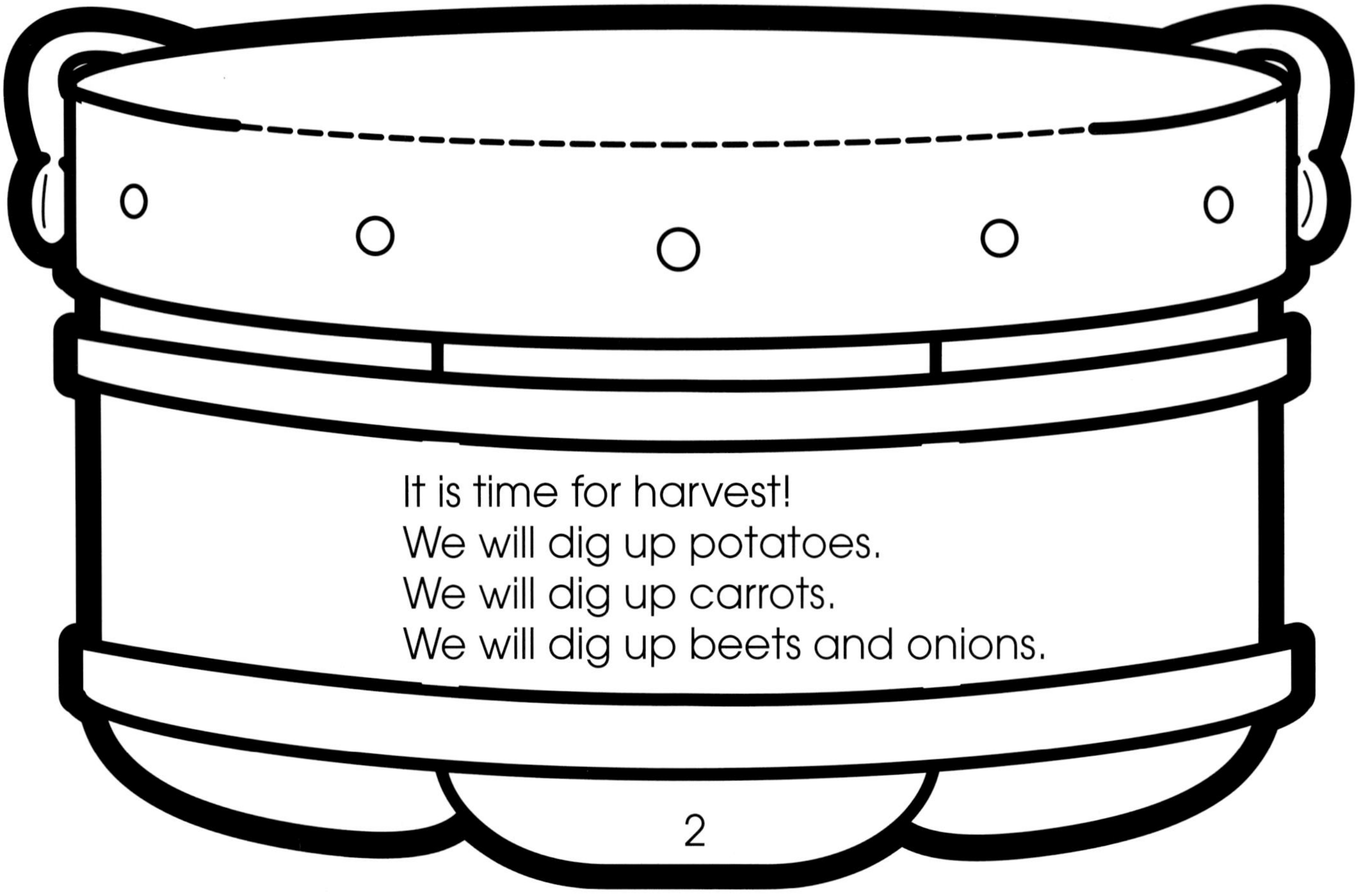

It is time for harvest!
We will dig up potatoes.
We will dig up carrots.
We will dig up beets and onions.
2

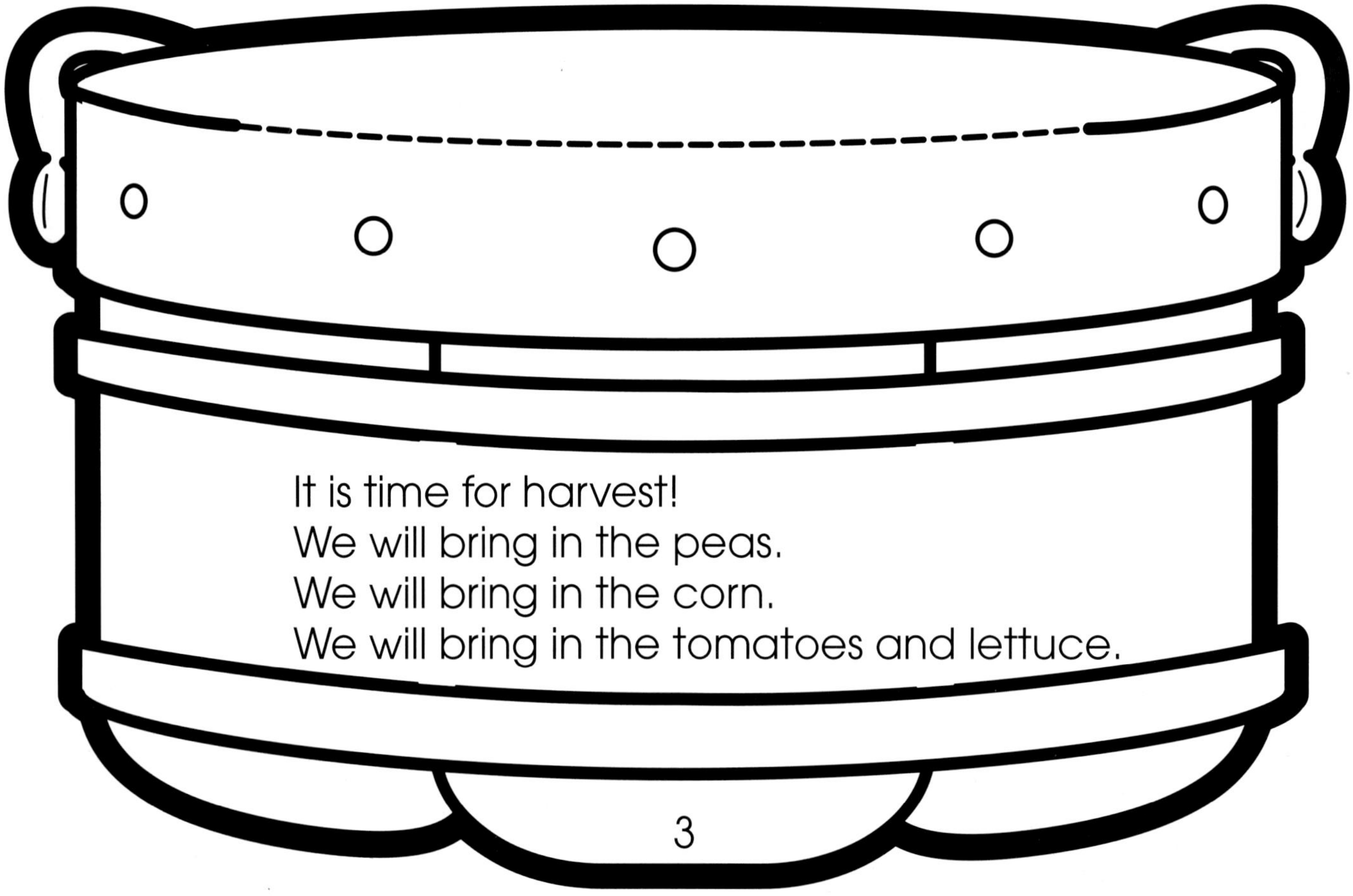

It is time for harvest!
We will bring in the peas.
We will bring in the corn.
We will bring in the tomatoes and lettuce.
3

 Note to the teacher: Use with "Time for Harvest!" on page 92.

Booklet Page and Patterns

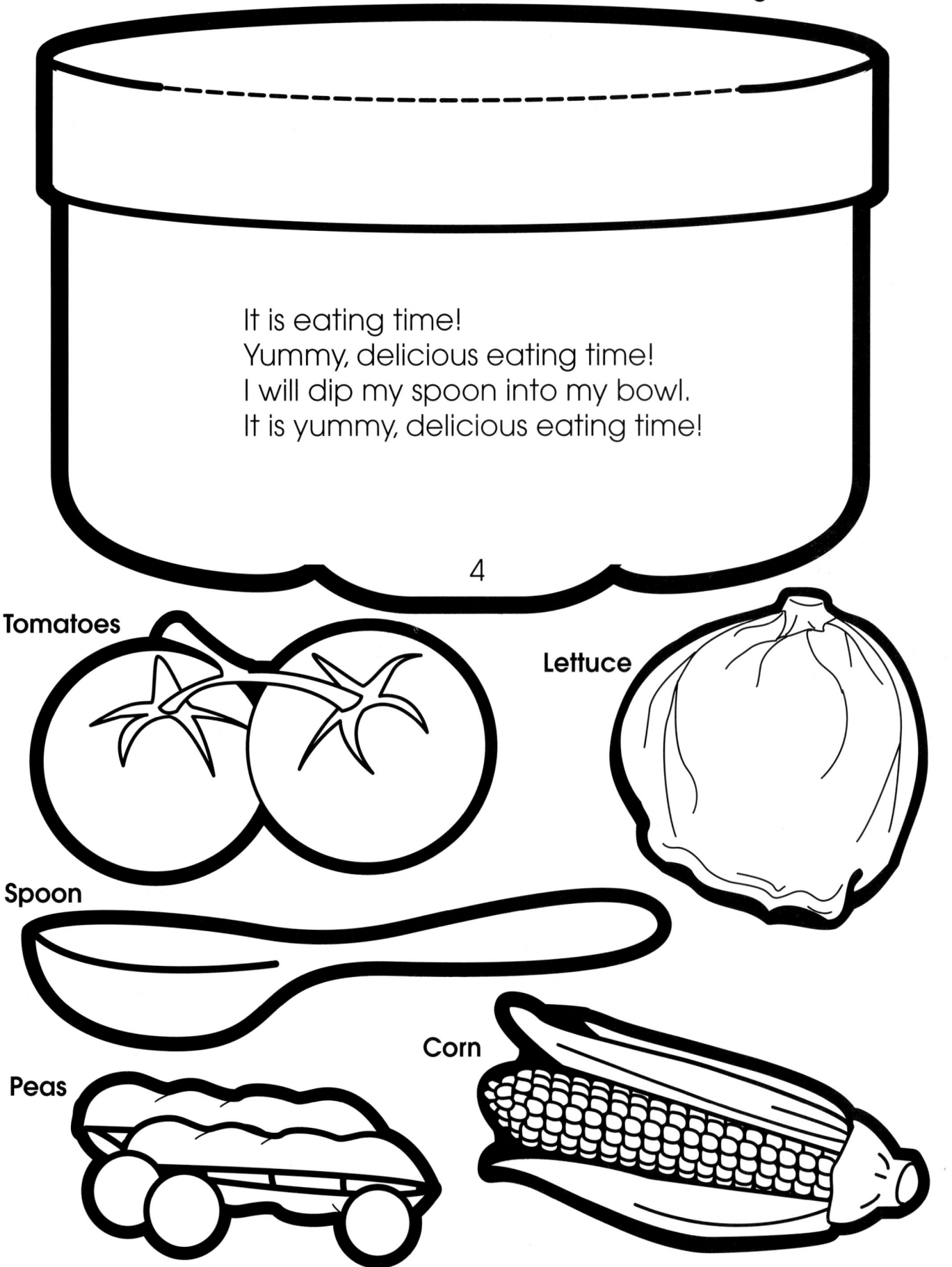

It is eating time!
Yummy, delicious eating time!
I will dip my spoon into my bowl.
It is yummy, delicious eating time!

4

Tomatoes

Lettuce

Spoon

Corn

Peas

©2000 The Education Center, Inc. • *I Can Make It! I Can Read It!* • Fall • TEC3509

Note to the teacher: Use with "Time for Harvest!" on page 92.

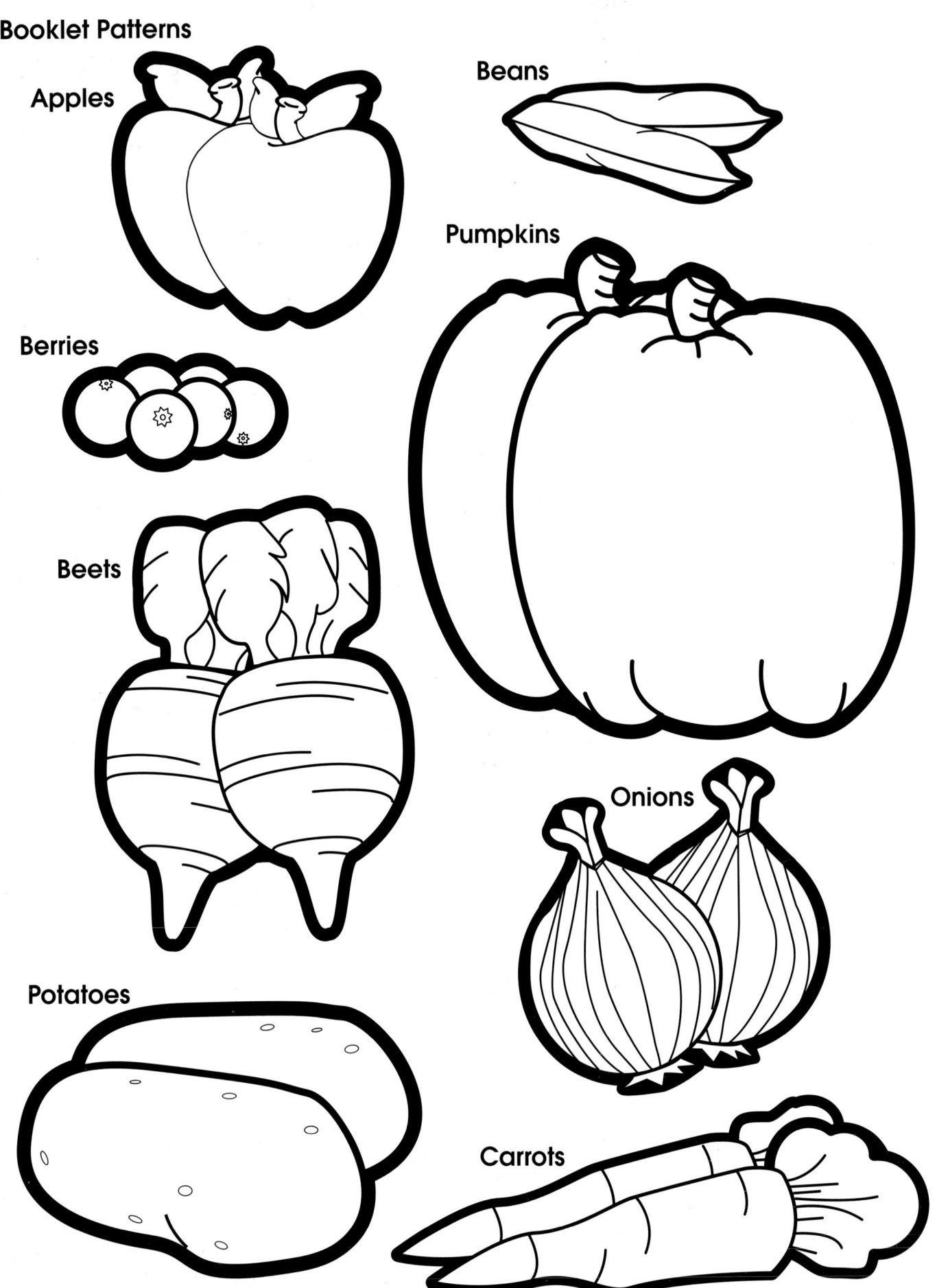